Fons&Porter® Presents

Quilts from The Henry Ford

24 Vintage Quilts Celebrating American Quiltmaking

Landauer Books

Fons & Porter® Presents
Quilts from
The Henry Ford

Copyright © 2005 by Landauer Corporation
Love of Quilting®, *Sew Easy*™ and *Sew Smart*™ are registered trademarks of Fons & Porter®

This book was designed, produced, and published by Landauer Books
A division of Landauer Corporation
3100 NW 101st Street, Urbandale, IA 50322
800-557-2144   www.landauercorp.com

President/Publisher: Jeramy Lanigan Landauer
Director of Operations: Kitty Jacobson
Editor in Chief: Becky Johnston
Creative Director: Laurel Albright
Art Director: Brian Shearer
Contributing Writer: Connie McCall
Contributing Technical Editor: Jean Nolte
Contributing Technical Writer: Rhonda Matus
Technical Illustrator: Linda Bender
Editorial Assistant: Debby Burgraff
Photographer: Craig Anderson Photography

Produced in association with **The Henry Ford**, Dearborn, Michigan.
The Henry Ford Editorial Team: Terri Anderson, Nancy EV Bryk, Wes Hardin and Toby Hines

All photographs from the collections of **The Henry Ford**, Dearborn, Michigan unless otherwise noted.

Craig Anderson Photography: Cover, 5,6,9,20,52,68,94,96,124,135,145,151,162,205

Cover: *Four Hearts* quilt, circa 1880s. Photographed in the bedroom of Bishop Milton Wright (father of Wilbur and Orville), Wright Home, Greenfield Village, Dearborn, Michigan.

Frontispiece: Henry Ford (1863–1947), photographed circa 1915.

Library of Congress Cataloging-in-Publication Data

Fons, Marianne.
    Fons & Porter presents quilts from **The Henry Ford**: 24 vintage quilts celebrating American quiltmaking.
      p. cm.
    Includes bibliographical references and index.
    ISBN 1-890621-91-9
    1. Patchwork--Patterns. 2. Quilting. 3. Quilts--United States--History. 4. McCord, Susan Noakes, 1829-1909.
    5. Henry Ford (Organization) I. Title: Quilts from **The Henry Ford.** II. Title: Fons and Porter presents quilts from **The Henry Ford**. III. Porter, Liz. IV. Title.

TT835.F6657 2005
746.46'041--dc22

                         2005051150
                    ISBN 13: 978-1890621-91-9
                    ISBN 10: 1-890621-91-9
             Hardcover ISBN 10: 0-9770166-1-7

This book is printed on acid-free paper.
Printed in China

10-9-8-7-6-5-4-3-2

the Henry Ford

Mission Statement

The Henry Ford provides unique educational experiences based on authentic objects, stories and lives from America's traditions of ingenuity, resourcefulness and innovation. Our purpose is to inspire people to learn from these traditions to help shape a better future.

Fons & Porter® Presents
Quilts from
The Henry Ford

contents

All of the quilts photographed on location in *Greenfield Village* were done so under the supervision of **The Henry Ford's** Conservation Department. Textile Conservator Fran Faile and her team first laid acid-free materials down on all painted, masonry or organic surfaces and (while wearing cotton gloves) carefully positioned every quilt for photography. Each outdoor quilt photograph has been digitally altered to remove any of the protective underlayments that may have still been visible.

From the President
The Henry Ford

In the early 1900s automotive pioneer Henry Ford and his wife Clara began collecting historical objects, vehicles and furnishings that ordinary folks had designed, produced and used during the previous two centuries.

Ford's goal was to create a different kind of museum that would tell the stories of ordinary people who did extraordinary things. The museum complex that Ford established in 1929—now known as **The Henry Ford** and including *Henry Ford Museum*, *Greenfield Village*, IMAX® Theatre, *Ford Rouge Factory Tour*, *Benson Ford Research Center*, and *Henry Ford Academy*—is today the nation's largest and most comprehensive history attraction.

From our founders, Henry, Clara, and Edsel Ford, to the present, **The Henry Ford** has maintained a consistent mission to honor, celebrate, and analyze America's deep tradition of resourcefulness, ingenuity, and innovation. Our intention is to inspire and help develop the next Thomas Edison, Henry Ford, Orville Wright, or Rosa Parks—all powerful innovators who changed the world and whose presence shapes this magnificent institution. Henry Ford created this museum and assembled its vast and diverse collections to honor, in his words, "the common genius of the American people." Perhaps the collection that most demonstrates this notion is our collection of American quilts. That is why we are delighted that this book is being published by Landauer Corporation, a firm whose passion for quilting and the preservation of historic quilt designs has inspired countless people to try their hand at "driving the needle" and to become active participants in this traditional American handcraft.

The patient artists who created the wonderful works of folk art featured in our collections have joined the pantheon of American innovators who "live" at **The Henry Ford** and whose work is waiting here to inspire you. I hope you enjoy the quilts in this volume and that you will come to **The Henry Ford** to invigorate your own innovative wellspring. Remember, ordinary people have changed the world. You can, too!

Steven K. Hamp
President

From the Curator
The Quilt Collection
at The Henry Ford

In their efforts to create a museum that would focus on the stories of how everyday Americans lived and worked in the past, Henry and Clara Ford began collecting on a massive scale.

This early accumulation included plain old wagons, grease lamps, toasters, tractors and threshing machines—the kinds of things few other millionaires would give a second thought. The Fords included quilts in their collecting endeavors and sought examples from all over the country. There was little question that quilts, often assembled from modest fabric scraps, epitomized the resourcefulness of American women that Henry Ford so admired.

Henry and Clara Ford's early twentieth-century quilt acquisitions formed the basis for our nationally significant collection of American quilts. Today, that collection numbers 250 and includes objects as diverse as whole cloth quilts made by farmwives in the 1700s to a bedcover created by a male tailor from army blankets and automobile pennants during World War I. Most of the pieces in our holdings were crafted by anonymous makers of whom very little personal information is known. But a few, such as the twelve quilts created by Indiana farmwife Susan McCord, came to us complete with photos and biographies of their makers. With the addition of 1970s Hawaiian quilts and 1990s bedcovers from the immigrant Hmong community, the curators at **The Henry Ford** have steadily expanded the collection so that it includes representations of the craft from the late twentieth century.

Visitors who examine our quilts on exhibit often remark that they cannot imagine how unschooled women acquired the math and design skills necessary to create these complex textiles. Experienced quilters, however, are not baffled; they find inspiration in the designs and immediately begin seeing ways to adapt and modify the patterns. We at **The Henry Ford** hope that everyone who studies and recreates the quilts featured in this volume develops an even deeper appreciation for the incredible resourcefulness, ingenuity, and innovation of the American quilter—individuals who quite literally were able to create something quite special from virtually nothing at all.

Nancy EV Bryk
Curator, Domestic Life

Fons&Porter® Presents
Quilts from The Henry Ford

We jumped at the opportunity, when invited by the publisher, to delve into the museum archives of **The Henry Ford** and choose twenty-four spectacular quilts to present with full instructions. We consider it an honor to connect with and present to you these landmarks of American quilting history.

From the time we discovered quilting in the mid-1970s, we grooved on antique quilts, quilt blocks, and fabric swatches from the past. We fell in love with the printed fabrics, the block designs, and the overall look of quilts from American quiltmaking history. We wanted such classic quilts for our all-American homes but, as young mothers, couldn't afford to buy them. Our passion for quilting was fueled by our desire to live day to day with traditional quilt styles. We learned to do patchwork and appliqué, both by hand and machine, in order to get what we wanted. Our newfound skills opened the world of quiltmaking to us and we've never looked back.

The magnificent designs created by the American women of the nineteenth and early twentieth centuries provide constant inspiration for us and for many other quilt enthusiasts who study the

patterns and styles of a bygone era and update them into perfect projects for today's avid quilt hobbyists. In the instructions for each of this book's projects, you'll find modernized methods for as much of the cutting and sewing as possible.

The curators and staff at **The Henry Ford** welcomed us with open arms and ushered us behind the scenes where the treasures of this great museum are safely kept. We thank them here for their warmth and generosity, and we urge you to make your own trip to Dearborn, Michigan, as we have, to see all that **The Henry Ford** has to offer!

About Fons & Porter®

Marianne Fons and Liz Porter met in a beginners quilting class in Winterset, Iowa, around 1976. Nestled in the heartland of the Midwest, Winterset is home to the famed Bridges of Madison County. Mothers of young children, they were looking for something to do that would "stay done." They found that quilting satisfied their souls and that teaching classes earned them "diaper money." At a time when very few books on quilting were available, they decided to write their own, and the partnership of Fons & Porter® was born.

One quilting book led to another, and another. Their 1993 *Quilter's Complete Guide,* published by Oxmoor House, is considered "the Bible of quiltmaking" and is still in print with more than 400,000 copies sold.

Since 1996, Marianne and Liz have been a popular presence on public television, co-hosting over 175 episodes of instructional quilting for audiences nationwide. Their program, "Fons & Porter's Love of Quilting," is the most widely aired quilting program available, reaching 82% of American households.

In 2001, Marianne and Liz had the opportunity to acquire their magazine, *Love of Quilting,* from Oxmoor House, a Time/Warner company. Under their direction, the magazine has grown to a circulation of over 250,000, making it the largest-circulated quilting magazine in the US.

Despite the growth of their business and its many responsibilities, what Marianne and Liz still love best is sitting down at a sewing machine, or with a needle and thread, and joining pieces of cotton cloth to make a beautiful quilt.

A Century of
Quilting Genius
1825–1925

Celebrating enduring works of art
created by women of ingenuity

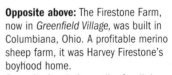

T he 24 quilts from **The Henry Ford** collection featured in the chapters that follow were made during an exciting transition period in American istory. The years from 1825 to 1925 marked a century f explosive growth in industry and technology.

Labor-saving inventions and dvances in technology during his vital century of progress ransformed the American scene rom a rural, agrarian society ocused almost solely on survival o a more comfortable era in vhich work could be combined with leisure activities and creative xpression such as quiltmaking.

Surprisingly enough, American vomen, whether they lived in the :ities or survived the hardship and leprivation of life on the frontier, he prairie, and later the nomestead, displayed amazing ngenuity and even genius in the quilts they made from scraps of :loth, using the most primitive of ools. Even the most basic utility quilts showed an originality in

composition, design and color that endures to today.

As the Industrial Revolution progressed, so did the quiltmaker's opportunity to exhibit greater strokes of quilting genius with the availability of affordable and far greater fabric choices, colorfast dyes, tools, and equipment such as the sewing machine. With the advent of modern conveniences— from cookstoves to electric lights—quiltmakers also enjoyed the luxury of a few more minutes of ease in their tedious workday to devote to quiltmaking, often leading to a passion for creating a practical work of art.

Using a palette of patchwork or appliqué for artistic expression, quiltmakers (almost always women) incorporated into their

designs the elements from the world in which they lived and worked. A flock of geese seen overhead inspired the Flying Geese block; a garden filled with flowers became the Grandmother's Flower Garden block. Logs overlapped to form a cabin's walls and corners became the foundation of the Log Cabin block, and a neighborhood barn raising soon made its way into textile history.

Henry Ford's exemplary vision for preserving pieces of the past— from quilts and cabins to working farms—aptly illustrates the American tradition of ingenuity, resourcefulness, and innovation.

On the pages that follow, discover for yourself history in the making of an enduring art form— the American quilt.

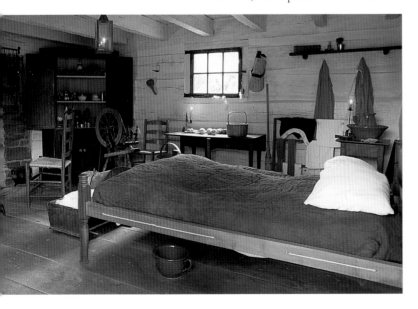

Opposite above: The Firestone Farm, now in *Greenfield Village,* was built in Columbiana, Ohio. A profitable merino sheep farm, it was Harvey Firestone's boyhood home.
Opposite inset: An appliqué quilt is draped over the porch rail of the Sarah Jordan Boarding House.
Left: The interior of William Holmes McGuffey's home circa 1800.
Top right: The center table in Noah Webster's House is covered with wife Rebecca's quilting paraphernalia.

Quilts and Culture
1825 -1850

The American Scene

The early years of the second quarter of the nineteenth century were dominated by unprecedented economic growth and expansion for the newly-formed United States of America. The spirit of adventure prevailed as families settled vast regions of uncharted territory—the Midwest, the Ohio Valley and the Mississippi Valley, and the Southeastern states.

Fueled by economic growth, transportation systems were developed as necessary ways to ship cotton and other crops and to get goods and supplies to settlers in the interior.

The Erie Canal, completed in 1825, offered a reverse means of transporting goods, out of the interior to the port at the heart of commerce—New York City.

The building of additional canal systems allowed steamboats to carry goods north and south. Known as the age of the steamboat, the years from 1820 to 1850 also brought the railroads that ultimately dominated the long-distance transportation scene.

Hearth and Home

Much of this migration, mostly westward, created both physical and emotional hardship—particularly for women who left family, friends, hearth and home for regions unknown. Quilts gave comfort.

Thick utility quilts were used to line the sides of covered wagons, to pad wagon seats, and to wrap dishes. At the end of the journey, quilts lined the walls of sod huts and log cabins. In desperation, women pressed quilts into service as substitutes for coffins to bury the dead, often children, who failed to survive the arduous journey. These frequent losses occasionally resulted in mourning quilts as mementos of lost loved ones.

Commemorative quilts whose blocks contained embroidered or even hand-written records of ceremonial events such as engagements, marriages and

Above: This bright appliqué album quilt may have been made by children circa 1850.
Left: Henrietta Johnson Wilson's circa 1850 quilt includes piecework and broderie perse floral chintz cut out and appliquéd in the corners of the star.

births emerged as tributes to the quiltmaker's needlework skills.

Elaborate Baltimore Album quilts were in vogue during this time. Probably made by a group called "Ladies of Baltimore," these quilts were often made and sold to raise money for worthy causes.

The Baltimore Album quilts carried the same sentiments that were expressed by friendship or commemorative quilts, but they also took the elements of broderie perse (*opposite*) to unprecedented heights.

Turkey red in prints and solids dominated with many additional prints used for layer upon layer of appliquéd baskets, fruits, flowers,

leaves, stems, birds and butterflies that filled the blocks. Often lavishly bordered with berries, blossoms, and intricate twining vines, many quilts were topped off with inked or stamped signatures.

Plain or fancy, quilt blocks gained popularity in part over whole-cloth and medallion-style quilts because of the limited space for quiltmaking in covered wagons and pioneer homes. Blocks also provided a means of sharing favorite patterns and reaching out to other women through "quiltings" or "quilting parties." In New England, quilting gatherings might be followed by dancing.

Top: The circa 1880 Firestone Farmhouse includes a sitting room used every day by the family for relaxing, reading, or small chores.
Below: *Godey's Lady's Book* featured this illustration of a lively quilting party in September 1849.

1825 -1850

Textiles of the Times

With so many practical uses for quilts, as well as the need for creative expression, the demand for fabric soared. Women who previously spent hours cleaning, carding, spinning, and weaving to make their own fabric had little opportunity for such time-consuming tasks.

The exploding textile industry rose to meet the demand. New England textile mills dominated the scene, creating thousands of job opportunities as they took over the spinning of yarn and the weaving of fabric—ultimately turning out millions of yards of printed fabrics. The invention of the roller printing cylinder reduced the former 15 hours needed to print a four-color design

on 50 yards of fabric to less than two minutes using the cylinder. Eliminating costly hand labor reduced the price of printed fabric dramatically, making it more affordable and fueling demand. By 1830, in fewer than 12 years, the cotton fabric industry's production grew from 92 million pounds to 300 million pounds.

In a trade industry formerly supplied by England and India, the textile industry in America employed a million and a half

workers by 1835. Thousands of men and women migrated to the New England mill towns seeking work in the factories.

Advances in fabric printing methods and the development of permanent dyes that yielded vibrant colors opened the way for the myriad of geometric designs for "calico" patterns.

This led to a plethora of choices for quiltmakers, who whole-heartedly welcomed the colorfast washable cottons.

Above: Sarah Jordan's Boarding House was a haven for Thomas Edison's bachelor employees.
Middle: Typically, copperplate-printed textiles are monochromatic, such as this circa 1800 example.
Below: A roller-printed cotton fabric from the 1840s.

Glossary

Broderie perse quilts – Medallion quilts that use motifs cut from a printed fabric and appliquéd onto a plain background; *broderie perse* is French for Persian embroidery.
Calico – Originally, any cotton fabric figured with one or more colors, either woven into the fabric, painted on, or printed. The name came from Calicut, the Indian port city that first produced these fabrics.
Chintz – From the Indian word *chint*, which means "variegated." Originally, painted or printed fabrics were referred to as chints. The terms "calico" and "chintz" were used interchangeably in the trade with India.
Palampore – A large cotton spread from India; painted and/or resist-dyed, especially in a Tree of Life or Flowering Tree motif.
Whole-cloth quilt – A quilt made from one large expanse of fabric (which could be pieced together), adorned only by a border if at all.

Calico

Chintz

Palampore

Whole-Cloth Quilt

Broderie perse

Prominent Dye Colors

Indigo Blue

Two plants, woad and indigo, were early sources of blue. In the 1700s, indigo became an important crop in the American South. Growers there increased indigo production until they were shipping more than a million pounds of indigo leaves to England each year for fabric dyes.

Yellow

Yellows were obtained chiefly from two spices, saffron and turmeric, and from the bark of the black oak. Chrome yellow, a mineral dye, was introduced in the United States in 1830. Antimony orange and chrome orange are also mineral dyes. Yellow was used with blue to make green and with red to make orange. Yellows from plants are fugitive: they fade away when exposed to light, leaving only the blue or the red. This fading is evident in quilts made before 1840 or 1850.

Brown

The browns used in American dyeing came primarily from butternut, black walnut, and logwood trees, usually from their bark. Logwood also could produce navy blue, which faded to light pink or purple. A mineral brown from manganese was accidentally produced in a search for a glaze; this manganese brown gave a range from light bronze to darker brown.

Turkey Red

In the eighteenth and nineteenth centuries, a plant called madder was the most frequently used source of red dye. However, madder also produced many shades of rose and purple, and it faded. Dyers knew that the Middle East had a secret process for a bright red that did not wash out. This dye was introduced in France as rouge Turc or rouge d'Adrianople—hence, Turkey red.

Fabric printing

Artisans in India used both hand painting and block printing to adorn their finely woven fabrics. When commercial trade blossomed during the 1600s, Indian calico, chintz, and palampore fabrics gained popularity in Europe.

Block printing was the earliest mechanical form of printing designs onto fabric. It was the European method of choice for about a century. Block printing could be done in four colors, with four separate blocks placed in register with each other.

Copperplate printing ruled until about 1830, when it was in turn supplanted by roller printing.

Roller printing was first patented in 1785 in Scotland, and development of roller printing led to the mass production of textiles.

Roller printing used copper cylinders, and printing was by the intaglio method. The design that was engraved into the cylinder was limited in size by the circumference of the cylinder; such a roller produced a design repeat every 15 or 16 inches. The cylinders rotate in a dye trough; each cylinder applies one color to the design. The early roller printers applied up to four colors. (Today we use rotary screen printing.) The roller printing process allowed for mass production with expanded design possibilities.

1825 - 1850

Milestones in Technology

Jacquard loom

The textile industry ushered in the Industrial Revolution. In England, there were many new advances. In 1733, John Kay invented the **flying shuttle**, and in 1764, James Hargreaves created the **spinning jenny**; this event was followed by

Spinning jenny

a patent for the spinning frame by Richard Arkwright in 1768.

In 1872, James Watt patented the **steam engine** which was used for running automated carding and spinning machines which had been water-driven. In 1779, Samuel Crompton invented the **spinning mule**; in 1785, Edmund Cartwright invented the **power loom**, and Claude Berthollet invented **chemical bleaching**.

The United States issued its first patent in 1790 to William Pollard of Philadelphia for a machine that could rove and spin cotton.

Eli Whitney is credited with the invention of a **cotton gin** in 1794; it eliminated much of the tedious process of cleaning short-staple

cotton (grown in the South), thus developing the basis for mass production. Taking his inspiration from copperplate printing used for printing fabric, Whitney made the correlation between engraving on a copper plate for many identical impressions, and making all the parts of a musket in multiples first, then assembling the parts—early mass production.

Cotton gin

At the turn of the century, Frenchman J.M. Jacquard invented the **Jacquard loom** which used punched cards to mechanically and affordably create more interesting and affordable patterns.

In 1844, John Mercer introduced **"mercerizing,"** a method of strengthening cotton and facilitating the fabric's ability to accept dyes. In 1849, Walter Hunt created the **safety pin**.

In 1850 Margaret Knight, at the age of 12, had an idea for a **stop-motion device** that could be used in textile mills to shut off machinery, preventing workers from being injured. Knight eventually received some 26 patents—her machine that made flat-bottomed bags is still in use.

And, throughout the second quarter of the nineteenth century, several inventors contributed to the design of a working **sewing machine** (see page 22).

Below: Turn-of-the-century sewing notions in Mrs. Cohen's Detroit Millinery Shop.

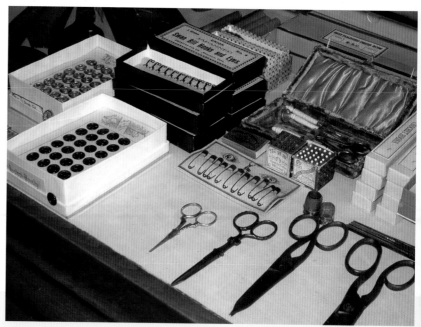

1825 – 1850

Pieces of the Past

Until the early 1800s, fabric was laboriously printed using wooden blocks cut with the design. However, by the 1830s, American calico printers largely abandoned this old process in favor of printing with engraved copper cylinders, using a separate cylinder for each color imprinted on the fabric. Featured here are typical prints found on album-type quilts of the mid-1800s.

Detail from a circa 1843 dress fabric

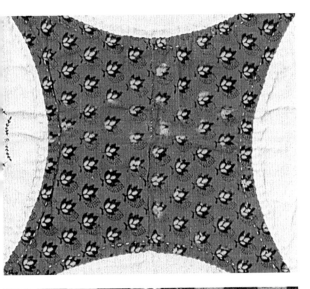

Detail from a circa 1845 one-way patterned printed cotton fabric

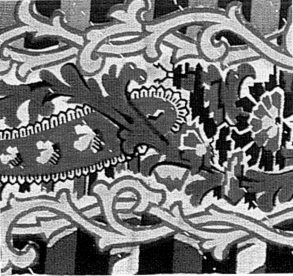

Two details from a roller-printed calico fabric from a circa 1846 quilt

Quilts and Culture
1850 - 1875

The American Scene

The Homestead Act of 1862 precipitated another vast migration of pioneers. Lured by the promise of prosperity, these brave souls fanned out across the prairies by horse and wagon to establish homesteads. Others headed farther west to California, Oregon and the Washington Territory in search of gold.

The expansion of federally subsidized railroads such as the Union Pacific-Central Pacific and Northern Pacific, which soon criss-crossed the country, greatly facilitated the movement of goods and services.

This migration necessitated goods and services, including an increased demand for such mundane items as bedding.

Midway through this third quarter of the nineteenth century, 1861 marked the beginning of the nation's Civil War. For four long years, the suffering nation was divided.

Mission and relief work took precedence over decorative sewing and quilting. Quilts were made for use on the battlefields or were raffled to raise funds through the efforts of an estimated 20,000 soldiers' aid societies. Fund-raising events were known as "sanitary fairs." The name is derived from the US Sanitary Commission, an organization responsible for handling volunteer contributions and supplies for the Union Army. From 1863 through 1865, large cities hosted the fairs, with the 1864 New York Metropolitan Fair netting an impressive $1.2 million for soldiers' aid.

Careful records kept by the US Sanitary Commission estimate that, as a result of these fairs, some 250,000 quilts and "comforts" were distributed by the Commission and other agencies.

Above and Left: Steam locomotives and railroads linked American communities large and small with the wider world and provided citizens with access to a wide array of manufactured goods. Railroad station, Petoskey, Michigan, 1908.

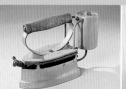

Cast iron flatiron, 1870–1900

Mrs. Potts type iron, 1893–1900

Gasoline-burning iron, circa 1908

x iron in swan design, 77–1890

Electric iron and trivet, circa 1905

Hearth and Home

The arduous task of maintaining self-sustaining homesteads required pioneer women to work from morning to night at a variety of menial and often back-breaking chores. Inevitably, Monday's laundry was followed by Tuesday's ironing, one of the toughest tasks of the homemaker's week. Pressing irons came in many sizes and shapes—full-size for general use, smaller for a child to learn on, and specialized for sleeves and collars or for pressing pleats or ruffles. A cast-iron trivet was a necessary accessory so the user could set the hot iron down.

The box iron had a hollow body that was filled with burning coals or charcoal or heated in the fireplace; it was lightweight, but it tended to get sooty.

Sad irons, so called because "sad" then meant "heavy" or "solid," could be heated on the stove and stayed clean. With sad irons, heavier was better, and using one was exceedingly hard work. The handle of the sad iron could cause bad burns unless the user wrapped a towel around it.

In 1871, Mrs. Mary Francis Potts of Ottumwa, Iowa, invented a removable wooden handle for the sad iron. Not only could the soleplate be heated on the stove and then a cool handle be attached, but a second iron could be heating on the stove and the user just changed the iron when the first one cooled down.

With the migration to cities, men became wage-earners. Women were afforded some leisure time, since luxuries such as water and sewage systems, electricity, and modern inventions like improved stoves and lamps made life easier. The shift from self-sustaining farms to earned incomes narrowed the woman's focus to maintaining a household. The new way of thinking was that women in general need not be concerned with the public world

of business or politics. Lydia Marie Child's *The American Frugal Housewife,* a popular advice book, and other publications such as *Progressive Farmer* and *Ladies' Home Journal* promoted the ideals of domesticity.

Quilts fit nicely with the domestic ideals of the time— among them the virtues of thrift (in use of scraps of fabric and in use of time) and the creation of a beautiful world by nurturing and serving others ("a man's home is his castle"). Quilts made for utility bedding, for causes such as the war effort, and for ceremonial occasions such as weddings, departures, or deaths were a socially accepted and applauded use of leisure time. They also provided a much-needed source of personal fulfillment and achievement for the quiltmakers.

Top: Ironing was wearisome, hot work. During the late 1800s and early 1900s a variety of innovations made irons safer and more convenient to use.

Above: This lovely wooden box is fitted for sewing tools for the genteel needleworker of the early-nineteenth century.
Left: Sarah Jordan's kitchen, as it may have looked about 1880, surely bustled with activity as she cooked and cleaned for Edison's bachelor employees.

19

Textiles of the Times

The log cabin was a cultural icon during this tumultuous period of American history. A symbol of modest beginnings, the log cabin was equated with the image of a self-made man who reached his goals through hard work but never forgot his humble roots.

Revered national heroes like Abraham Lincoln were born in these rustic shelters. In 1840, William Henry Harrison centered his successful presidential campaign around the image of the log cabin. The candidate was portrayed as a common man with a desire to live his life in a log house in the woods. Cabins became props in parades and rallies and were even the theme of

Above: McGuffey School, built in Greenfield Village in 1934, serves as a backdrop for the Barn Raising Log Cabin Quilt in the foreground.
Below right: Window panes in log cabins (such as this one from McGuffey Birthplace in Greenfield Village) are said to have inspired the quilt's red center block, which according to folklore represented warmth from a fireplace or light from a window.
Opposite top: Variations of the Log Cabin quilt include 3D Diamonds, Courthouse Steps, Straight Furrow, Barn Raising, and Zigzag.

popular songs. During this time, Horace Greeley published a weekly pro-Whig newspaper, aptly called *The Log Cabin.*

Logs were also a symbol of man's conquest over the wilderness. They represented trees cut down and fashioned into useful dwellings. American landscape painter Thomas Cole

painted various works during the 1840s, paintings in which a cabin carved out of the forest symbolized a new nation built by diligence and hard work.

During this era, sometime around the start of the Civil War, the Log Cabin quilt block pattern emerged. Beginning with a center square in red or yellow, representing warmth and light (often referred to as the "chimney"), fabric strips (logs) are

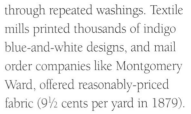

overlapped so that half the square is of light-colored logs and the other half is composed of dark. Numerous variations on the theme refer to events and icons of the time—from Barn Raising and Straight Furrow to Courthouse Steps and Streak of Lightning.

Indigo blue and white were at the height of popularity in the 1860s. Manufacturer John Hewson promoted the durability of indigo dye, which appealed to the practicality of his customers who wanted fabrics that kept their color

Left: Blue-and-white quilts, of simple and inexpensive cottons, produced beloved quilts like this circa 1880 summer spread. **Below:** An upstairs bedroom in Sarah Jordan's circa 1880 Boarding House includes a sturdy Log Cabin quilt in a variation of the 3D Diamonds pattern.

through repeated washings. Textile mills printed thousands of indigo blue-and-white designs, and mail order companies like Montgomery Ward, offered reasonably-priced fabric (9½ cents per yard in 1879).

During these economic growth years, early department stores such as R. H. Macy's and John Wanamaker's counted on the railroads as a reliable source of freight delivery. And, with reliable product delivery, mail order companies like Sears Roebuck, and Co. and Montgomery Ward could fill even the most rural home with an inviting cornucopia of piece goods and tools—from dress to upholstery prints and patterns—and with tools like a sewing machine.

The invention and refinement of the sewing machine had a great impact on the textile industry by increasing the demand for fabric to unprecedented levels. Mass production of linens, from bedding to tablecloths, made life easier for women, since sewing and mending were constant parts of daily life for the homemaker. When the sewing machine went into wide production in the late 1850s, it was a much coveted timesaver.

Newfound freedom from tedious hand sewing of the family wardrobe permitted more time for fancy stitching and exploration of new quiltmaking techniques such as appliqué, complex geometric shapes, and borders, all made easier by the use of the sewing machine.

21

1850-1875

Milestones in Technology

The Sewing Machine

Isaac Singer was one of the first to build a successful sewing machine. Singer's inventiveness, paired with the business acumen of Edwin Clark, changed the lives of American women, relieving them of the time-consuming and eye-straining drudgery of hand-stitching the family's clothing.

Many inventors had seen the need. In the United States, Walter Hunt built a somewhat successful sewing machine in 1834 but did not patent it for fear that it would put seamstresses out of work. (Hunt later invented the safety pin and a variety of other items.)

In 1846, Elias Howe invented the first workable sewing machine with a lockstitch, which he patented. In 1849 and 1850, ten more sewing machine patents were issued.

Isaac Singer and businessman Edwin Clark began working together when Elias Howe sued Singer for infringement of his patent on the lockstitch. (Settlement of the suit eventually made Howe a wealthy man.) Clark saw in the penniless Singer a mechanical genius, and he agreed to provide free legal and financial advice in exchange for a third of the sewing machine business.

Singer continued to improve his machine, adding a foot-operated treadle to free the sewer's hands. The Singer machine was the first to have a needle that moved up and down and the first to be built into a furniture-style cabinet.

On his side of the partnership, Clark developed a stunning business innovation. A heavy sewing machine for commercial use cost $125. By making the machines for home use lighter, Singer got the price down to $50, but even this was not affordable for most families. Clark instituted the first installment payment plan, offering customers a sewing machine for as little as $5 down and $3 a month for 16 months. Sales zoomed; during the 1870s there was a year when Singer sold 600,000 sewing machines. Clark also established a network of salesrooms, instructors, and repair service.

Another sewing machine innovator was a woman, Helen Augusta Blanchard. In 1873, she patented a machine that made a zigzag stitch for finished seams and sturdier garments.

These commercial-grade sewing machines were a boon to the ready-to-wear industry.

For American women, the impact of the lighter, home sewing machine was remarkable. The 14 hours needed to sew a man's shirt by hand were reduced to an hour by machine.

Changes in use of time were accompanied by changes in fashions, as the sewing machine enabled women to sew dresses of complex construction and a shapely fit. Leftover pieces of fabric were not wasted—they went straight to the best source of quilting pieces—the scrap bag.

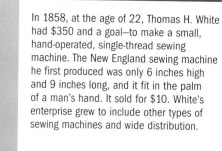

In 1858, at the age of 22, Thomas H. White had $350 and a goal—to make a small, hand-operated, single-thread sewing machine. The New England sewing machine he first produced was only 6 inches high and 9 inches long, and it fit in the palm of a man's hand. It sold for $10. White's enterprise grew to include other types of sewing machines and wide distribution.

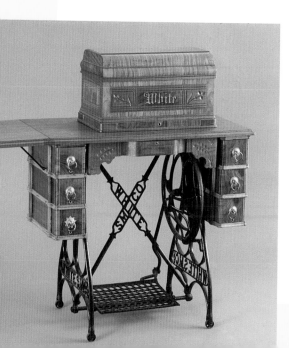

1850-1875

Pieces of the Past

Cotton fabric production—from spinning to dyeing—was so lucrative it was said that everywhere water ran quickly in New England, a mill sprang up. By the mid-1800s dozens of American textile mills were producing hundreds of fabrics for the average householder. Women could choose from an array of patterns and colors. Cotton was so much easier to clean and so inexpensive that women could afford more dresses than ever before.

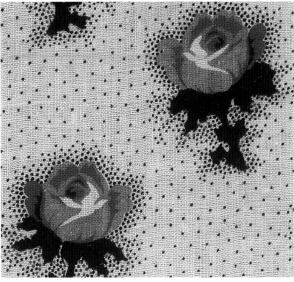

Detail from a circa 1870 calico fabric

Detail from a circa 1870 paisley print fabric

Detail from a circa 1870 calico fabric

Detail from a circa 1855 calico ruffle

23

Quilts and Culture
1875 - 1900

The American Scene

The fourth-quarter of the nineteenth century began with spectacular national centennial celebrations such as the Philadelphia Exposition, which opened on May 10, 1876, and drew huge crowds. Well over 100,000 people came to see such attractions as the massive Corliss steam engine. At 700 tons and 40 feet high, it could generate 2,500 horsepower, powering the

hundreds of machines in the fourteen-acre Machine Hall. Demonstrations such as this were tributes to the new Industrial Revolution that was transforming the United States into a recognized world power.

During this time, a transition of another sort was taking place.

The public school system was developed to provide free education to rich and poor alike. An amazing 15 million pupils attended public schools in 1898.

In his childhood, Henry Ford was among the American boys and girls whose values and outlook were shaped by the work of William Holmes McGuffey, the man whose last name became synonymous with "Reader." In fact, Ford considered McGuffey to

be the man most responsible for teaching industry and morality to America. The *McGuffey Eclectic Readers* ("eclectic" because their material came from many different sources) are often described as the books that probably exerted more influence on the literary tastes and moral values of several generations of young Americans than any other book except the Bible. Through many editions and several publishers, some 122 million copies of the *McGuffey Eclectic Readers* had been sold by 1920. (The books are still available in modern reprints and offered for sale in gift shops at **The Henry Ford.**)

Hearth and Home

Although most women were still at home, public school education and the establishment of the land grant colleges provided women with increased opportunities beyond the confines of hearth and

Opposite: McGuffey School was built in *Greenfield Village* by Henry Ford in 1934 for the students attending his Edison Institute Schools. Its schoolmaster's desk was made from the McGuffey's walnut kitchen table.
Below: Although there are few surviving "little red school houses," the quilt block they inspired remains one of America's favorite patterns.

home. Women's colleges such as Smith, Bryn Mawr, and others were established during this quarter century. Education soon offered alternatives to women, affording them the opportunity to work in socially sanctioned careers especially teaching, nursing and social work.

Textiles of the Time

An unexpected result of the Centennial Exposition in Philadelphia's Fairmount Park was the craze for anything Japanese. A record 9½ million people toured the Japanese pavilion and fell in love with the fluid design elements of the art—particularly the Japanese folding fan.

Japanese fan design coupled

with the sunflowers and lilies that were symbols of the sweeping Aesthetic Movement, ushered in a new quilting fad—crazy patchwork created from scraps of fancy fabrics and lavished with detailed embroidery. Silk manufacturers fueled the fad, seizing the opportunity to sell scraps that would otherwise have been discarded.

As with the earlier album quilts, crazy quilts offered an easy way to showcase bits of treasured fabric saved from ceremonial garments, such as wedding dresses and commemorative ribbons from fairs, exhibitions, and military or political campaigns.

Top left and right: In the late 1890s, widow Elizabeth Cohen made her living decorating women's hats in this building, originally located in Detroit. Elizabeth and her young family lived above the store.
Left: Rich, dark Japanese textiles and Asian folding fans may have inspired this variation of a *Fancy Crazy Fan* quilt, circa 1890 (see page 198).

25

1875-1900
Milestones in Technology

Electricity

One of the greatest discoveries of all time—how to generate and distribute electricity—fueled the passion for sewing and quilting.

The first widely-used electric appliance, the iron, was patented

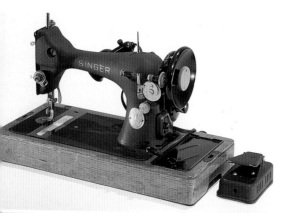

in 1882, but it was slow to catch on. Electricity was prohibitively expensive. Few homes were wired; a multitude of small generating companies served large stores, hotels, and city rail lines.

In 1893, when the brilliant lights of Chicago's Columbian Exposition dazzled the world, Thomas Edison's former business manager Samuel Insull was president of Chicago Edison. A visionary, Insull foresaw nation-wide electrification—if the cost could come down. Over a period of years, he consolidated the generating plants, changed the pricing structure for electricity

to lower its cost, and began an aggressive campaign to wire whole neighborhoods.

Insull also ran an advertising campaign with the message that electric appliances will set women free from drudgery. Making the electric iron a centerpiece of his campaign, he sent more than 100 salesmen door to door to offer free electric irons for six-month trials—in exchange for the old irons. Women by the thousands turned in their sad irons, and the electric iron was in.

The electric iron was soon followed by the electric sewing machine, patented in 1905, and then by dozens of other electric-powered conveniences.

Top right: In 1896, in his spare time, while Henry Ford was chief engineer at the Edison Electric Illuminating Company in Detroit, he produced a gasoline-powered auto he called a "quadricycle."

Upper left: A lucky housewife might purchase an electrified sewing machine in the early 1900s, requiring neither hand nor foot power for operation.

Lower left: Henry Ford's great hero was Thomas Edison, who met Ford at an engineers' convention and encouraged Ford in his automotive pursuits. In gratitude, Henry Ford dedicated his museum complex to Thomas Edison in 1929. Here, the two great men compare a 1930 light bulb with a replica of the first successful bulb from 1879.

Below: An electric iron circa 1910—it did not have to be heated on the kitchen stove!

1875 -1900

Pieces of the Past

The cost of American textiles made in New England, dropped every decade as the industry became more sophisticated, productive and competitive. All but the poorest could afford to purchase these inexpensive dress and shirting fabrics by the turn of the century. Previously, quilts had often been made from old clothes, but now calico was inexpensive enough that many were made with new fabrics purchased from the store. Natural dyes were being replaced by chemically-derived coal tar dyes.

Detail from a circa 1895 dress fabric

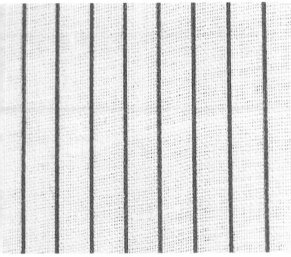

Detail from a circa 1880 shirting fabric

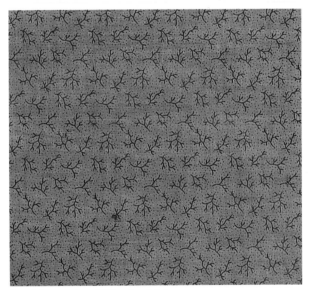

Detail from a circa 1890 calico fabric

Detail from a circa 1880 shirting fabric

Quilts and Culture
1900 -1925

The American Scene

A quarter-century of progress culminating in the "Roaring Twenties" was dominated by the automobile. From its introduction in the late 1890s, the automobile provided individuals with a level of personal mobility greater than any they had previously obtained from other forms of transportation. Manufacturers observed how the moving assembly line enabled Ford Motor Company to increase production while reducing costs, and quickly adapted the technique to produce a variety of consumer goods at more affordable prices.

Political developments in Europe led to "The Great War," which dominated the country's attention and resources during the First World War years of 1917 and 1918.

Relief committees were formed to make practical, serviceable quilts that were widely referred to as Liberty Quilts. Women's magazines offered patterns for these quilts, which as in Civil War days were often auctioned to raise funds for the war effort. Other fund-raising, autographed quilts were raffled by the Red Cross for hospital supplies and by the Women's Christian Temperance Union (WCTU) to wage war on alcoholism. Signature quilts were a double blessing for such charitable organizations. In this century-old fundraiser, the individuals who signed the quilts donated money (the center block signature commanded the highest fee) and the quilt itself brought in additional dollars when it was sold or raffled.

Hearth and Home

Due to advances in transportation, education, and labor-saving inventions, women's horizons were expanding beyond the limits of the previous century.

With the right to vote that was enacted in 1919 came more opportunities for women in business and commerce. The Jazz Age ushered in a new era of freedom from corsets, and especially for the "flappers," who wore makeup and donned bathing costumes for trips to the seashore in the family automobile.

Desire for new products was so great that many manufacturers encouraged consumers to buy "on time" to achieve the new standard of living by purchasing through installment plans.

Textiles of the Time

At the height of its popularity, the crazy quilt was a huge influence on quiltmaking, but the fad quickly faded and gave way to the traditional patchwork of the Colonial Revival.

Above: Army tailor Herbert James Smith sewed this quilt from machine-embroidered wool pennants representing various armed forces units during World War I.
Left: Inexpensive Model Ts increased car ownership in America. Here, automobiles fill the busy main street of Henderson, Texas, in 1920.

Advances in printing and distribution gave rise to the popularity of printed patterns, which were featured in magazines such as *Good Housekeeping* and *The National Stockman and Farmer*.

Exchanges of pattern names and designs led to standardization of such enduring patterns as the Log Cabin, Double Wedding Ring, Star of Bethlehem, Pineapple, Peony and Postage Stamp.

The Ladies' Art Company, which was started in St. Louis by a German immigrant family, offered more than five hundred quilt designs before it stopped publishing patterns in 1928.

In addition to the published patterns they bought, quiltmakers continued to share favorite block patterns for cotton patchwork, designs passed down from past generations of friends and family—and varied through time. The Amish developed a unique style of quilts based on their religious beliefs.

In addition to making quilts that would have perceived value for fund-raising, women also continued to make quilts for personal use. Quilting took on a new dimension early in this quarter-century when quilters became "competitive" in their attempt to use the smallest pieces possible to make quilts.

In the quilts, some twentieth-century quilters made blocks that were reduced to miniature one-inch squares composed of eight triangles, or to hexagons

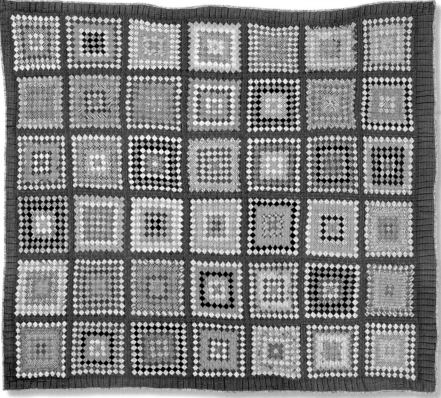

pieced from six tiny triangles. Postage Stamp quilts and variations required thousands of tiny squares and eventually caught the attention of the press. In later years, as competition increased, a Postage Stamp quilt from Iowa made history with 69,649 pieces—but it was soon topped by a quilt from Nebraska that boasted 87,789 individual pieces of fabric.

Top: Log Cabin *Zigzag* Variation (circa 1890), *Double Wedding Ring* (circa 1920), *Star of Bethlehem* (circa 1850), Log Cabin, *Pineapple* Variation (circa 1880), and an appliqué *Peony* pattern (circa 1850).
Center: This remarkable *Postage Stamp* quilt (circa 1925), made from tiny pieces of cotton, won an award at the 1927 Alabama State Fair (see page 195).
Right: *Ladies' Home Journal* began publication in 1883, chock full of articles on home and child care, knitting, sewing, home decoration and—as seen in this 1907 fashion issue—clothing styles.

1900-1925
Milestones in Technology

The Automobile

As a boy growing up just after the Civil War, Henry Ford was expected to become a farmer like his father. But Henry was fascinated by the mechanical world. At 13, he saw a self-powered steam tractor and knew he wanted to work with machines. Three years later, he left the farm and headed for the machine shops of Detroit.

In 1893, Henry became chief engineer of the Edison Illuminating Company's Station A, in charge of the plant's steam-powered generators. He was now 30; he was married and had a small child. This job could have been his career. But reading about gasoline-powered vehicles got Henry intrigued with the idea of building one.

Automobiles were appearing on American streets. Most ran on steam or electricity; a few had internal combustion engines that burned gasoline. Built one at a time, these early cars were affordable only for the wealthy. Henry Ford wanted to change that. Over the next three years, he spent his spare time building a car in the shed behind the house he was renting. Co-workers at the power plant helped Henry design and make every part of the 500-pound "Quadricycle," so named for its four oversized bicycle-type spoked wheels. The Quadricycle had a four-horsepower, two-cylinder engine; it had no reverse gear and no brakes. But it went 20 miles an hour, and on June 4, 1896, Henry successfully drove his homemade car through the streets of Detroit.

Several men were successfully designing and manufacturing steam- or electric-powered cars. Others, like Ransom Olds and the Duryea Brothers, would soon be producing gasoline-powered vehicles and setting-up dealerships. Henry wondered if he could become one of them.

In August 1896, Henry received encouragement from an unexpected source. His boss took him to Edison Illuminating Company's annual convention in Atlantic City, where he was introduced to Thomas Edison—the world's greatest inventor. Edison had already heard about this young employee's gasoline-powered car and asked to meet him. As Henry was describing the car, Edison suddenly banged his fist on the table and shouted, "Young man, that's the thing!" After listing the advantages of gas engines, Edison said emphatically, "You have the thing. Keep at it!" Henry later wrote, "That bang on the table was worth worlds to me."

In 1899, Henry set up the Detroit Automobile Company. That year, the nation's 57 automakers produced more than 3,700 cars. Henry's company failed after just 14 months. After building a successful race car, Henry tried again, founding the Henry Ford Company in 1901. This company started well, but Henry resigned in 1902 because his partners wanted to market expensive cars to wealthy customers. Henry's goal was to build a less expensive car aimed at the masses.

In 1903, Henry established Ford Motor Company. Its first product, the Model A, was a big success. Over the next four years, Henry introduced a succession of "alphabet cars": Models B, C, F, K, N, R and S. Henry's dream of a car that was rugged enough to handle America's roads, powerful enough to meet the needs of both farmers and city dwellers, simple to operate, and priced so almost anyone could afford it was realized in 1908 with the Model T—the car that over the next 19 years would put the world on wheels.

Above: E.K. Barker and wife in their 1903 Ford Model A (photo taken in 1915).
Left: Henry Ford standing next to the 10 Millionth Ford Model T (built in 1924), and the first car he ever made, the 1896 Quadricycle.

1900 -1925

Pieces of the Past

Some of the dark, saturated colors used in calicoes in the late 1800s were replaced with lighter, brighter pastels in the early 1900s. Many of these fabrics could be purchased from the general stores in small communities; Henry Ford purchased three of these fabrics from the unsold stock of old stores.

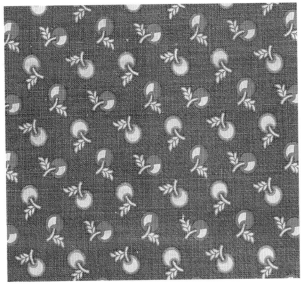

Detail from a circa 1920 fruit print fabric

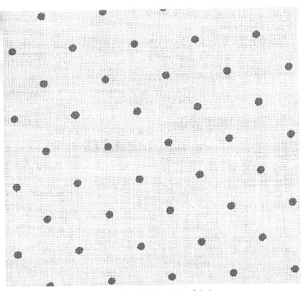

Detail from a circa 1910 printed dot calico fabric

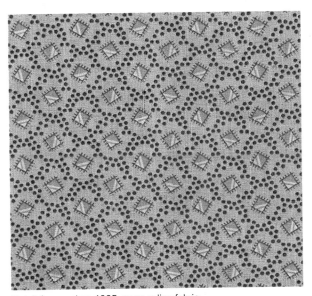

Detail from a circa 1925 green calico fabric

Detail from a circa 1900 Rococo Revival-style printed cotton fabric

Quilt Timeline

The numerous quilts in **The Henry Ford** textile collection represent years of careful consideration by the curatorial staff. Quilting experts Marianne Fons and Liz Porter (Fons & Porter®) worked with curator Nancy EV Bryk and her staff to select 24 quilts from this delightful array of color, pattern, texture and technique, quilts that would appeal to quilters of all skill levels—from the very beginner to the most experienced. Fons & Porter® introduce each of the 24 quilts with their reasons for choosing that quilt as a project for quilters to make. Complete how-to instructions and full-size patterns for the quilts are presented in a format that is familiar to readers of their *Love of Quilting*® magazine.

On the following pages, a timeline corresponding to *A Century of Quilting Genius: 1825–1925* is an informative reference guide for the historical context of the 24 quilts featured as projects— impressive examples of quilts that have withstood the test of time.

McCord Vine Quilt circa 1850

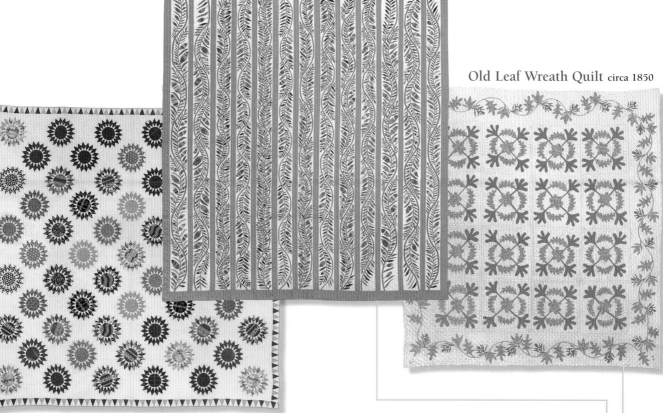

Old Leaf Wreath Quilt circa 1850

unburst Quilt circa 1840

825 1830 1835 1840 1845 1850

el Variation Quilt circa 1846

Star of Bethlehem Quilt circa 1850

Peony Quilt circa 1850

33

McCord Floral Urn Harrison Rose Quilt circa 1860

Feather with Flowers Quilt circa 1860-1890

1850   1855   1860   1865   1870   1875

Laurel Leaf Cross Quilt circa 1860

Straight Furrow Quilt circa 1870-1880

ur Hearts Quilt circa 1870-1900

Sunshine & Shadow Quilt circa 1880

Sunburst Medallion Quilt circa 1890

Barn Raising Variation Quilt circa 1880

3D Diamonds Quilt circa 1880

875 1880 1885 1890 1895 1900

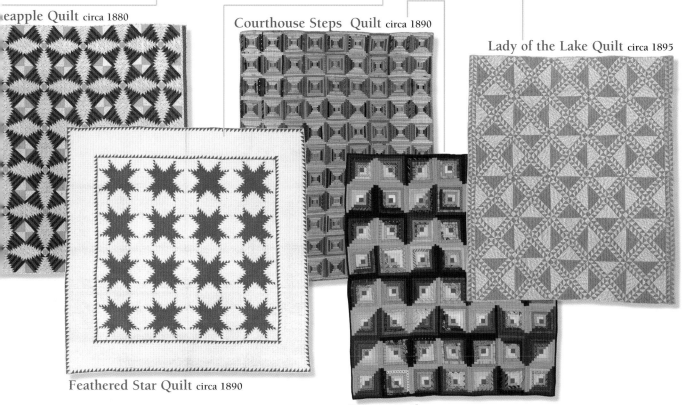

eapple Quilt circa 1880

Courthouse Steps Quilt circa 1890

Lady of the Lake Quilt circa 1895

Feathered Star Quilt circa 1890

Zigzag Quilt circa 1890

Double Wedding Ring Quilt circa 1920

Fancy Crazy Fan Quilt circa 1900

1900 1905 1910 1915 1920 1925

Postage Stamp Quilt circa 1925

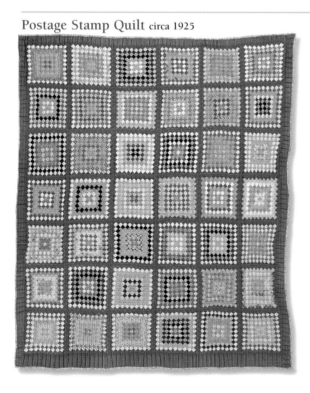

Rose Tree Quilt circa 193⬛

Susan McCord's Quilts:
A Farmwife's Legacy

Susan Noakes McCord (1829–1909) was an Indiana farmwife who bore seven children, loved to garden, and quilted for over fifty years. Like other quilters, she drew from her extensive bag of fabric scraps—choosing patterns, colors and techniques to make her quilts. But Susan McCord put all these elements together in ways that were highly original. The pages that follow offer an in-depth study of an ordinary farmwife with extraordinary quilting genius.

A Farmwife's Legacy

by Nancy EV Bryk, Curator, Domestic Life

Nineteenth-century American quilts are often considered the epitome of the seamstress' aesthetic expression. We are bewitched by the creations of industrious, and often anonymous, housewives. The finest quilted bedcovers dazzle us with colorful pattern, intricate construction, and exquisite workmanship. The twelve quilts made by Indiana farmwife Susan McCord (1829–1909) in the collections of Henry Ford Museum are among the very best of the genre. These quilts are representative examples of typical midwestern quilting in terms of fabric use, color scheme and technique. On another level, however, Mrs. McCord manipulated fabric, color and designs even on her quilts of traditional patterns, producing bedcovers that were far from ordinary. Finally, the McCord quilts of original design, master-fully engineered and executed, are extraordinary examples of American quiltmaking.

Unlike so many quilts in museum collections, in this case we are able to associate a face and personal history with the products. Susannah Noakes was born October 7, 1829, probably in Decatur County, Indiana.

Susannah, known as Susan, married schoolteacher Green McCord, an Ohio native, in 1849. They moved to Iowa and began farming, but soon returned to Indiana, settling in McCordsville, a small town east of Indianapolis that had been founded by one of Green's relatives. The McCords spent the rest of their lives on an eighty-acre farm in McCordsville. In the 1902 county atlas, Green was hailed as an early settler and a prominent community member. He is listed as an Oddfellow, church elder, and Civil War veteran, and is described as a staunch Republican.

What we know of Susan McCord is revealed through family reminiscences. This tiny bundle of energy bore seven children. Like most farmwives, she was responsible for the homestead's dairy and poultry. She was a devoted member of the McCordsville Methodist Episcopal Church, reading her Bible through each year and participating in church social activities such as sewing bees. Susan loved gardening and practiced homeopathic medicine, using tree barks, roots, and plants for healing. She sewed clothing for her flock of children, knitted accessories, embroidered bedsheets, produced decorative wreaths of human hair, and made at least thirteen bed quilts (three remain in private collections).

Susan McCord is representative of many nineteenth-century homemakers who were expected to raise a family, run a homestead, and provide "fancy work" for the home. Such homemade goods saved the family money, personalized the home, and displayed a farmwife's artistic talents. Writers Henry Williams and Mrs. C. S. Jones in *Beautiful Homes* (1878) urged housewives to create lovely items for their dwellings, believing that "taste dwells in unity with utilities and love."

When women like Susan McCord found the time to construct such goods remains a wonder. However, the 1820 edition of *The American Frugal Housewife* captured the essence of these industrious women's lives: "The true economy of housekeeping is simply the art of gathering up all the fragments so that nothing be lost. I mean the fragments of time, as well as materials. Nothing should be thrown away so long as it is possible to make any use of it."

Like other economical housewives of the era, Susan McCord sewed her quilts from material she had on hand, primarily clothing scraps. The fabrics include roller-printed cotton calicoes and turn-of-the-century wool flannel or dress velvets. Some pieces were cut from already well-worn clothing, while others appear to have been unused prior to inclusion in quilt tops. The backings of her quilts were often pieced from small muslin scraps, some no bigger than an inch or two on a side. There are no fancy imported furnishing chintzes found in these quilts. Most of her quilts are very thin and have little "filler," to provide warmth. Susan may have used these pieces as warm-weather bedcovers or "summer" quilts. What filling is included in these quilts is cotton batting, full of cotton hulls and debris. A frugal farmwife like Susan likely purchased inexpensive batting.

Examining the fabric, techniques, and patterns tells

us that the ten quilts were constructed as early as 1860 and as late as 1900. They are representative of a variety of popular, late-nineteenth-century quilts. The earliest ones are the two urn appliqué quilts (see Quilt Gallery), so–called because the primary design (urns) was applied to the surfaces, and stitched in place. These two were sewn about 1860 and feature the large floral motifs and red and green appliqué color scheme popular at mid-century. One urn appliqué features the Indiana pattern "Harrison

Below: From left: Family members are Millie McCord Canaday, daughter of Susan and Green; Green McCord; Ruth Canaday, Susan's granddaughter and the woman from whom Henry Ford Museum acquired the quilts; and Susan McCord. This is the McCord homestead in McCordsville, Indiana. Their eighty acres of farmland included a log cabin that served as their home for many years. Once they could afford it, the family replaced the log house with the fine frame home pictured here. A 1902 history of the county called the McCord frame house "...a paradise (compared to the log home) and a pride to the surrounding country, all the result of (Green's) personal labor and indefatigable industry."

Photograph courtesy of Mrs. Ruth Canaday McKesson

rose," named for William Henry Harrison, Indiana Territory's first governor and the United States' ninth president.

Susan's four pieced quilts, sometimes called "patchwork" in the ladies' magazines of the day, range in date from 1870 to the turn of the century. All are of well-known patterns and exhibit the pink and green color scheme common late in the century. She also constructed three turn-of-the-century "crazy" quilts, pieced bedcovers of dark, rich, heavy fabrics constructed in blocks of seemingly random arrangement, all the rage in the 1880s.

While Susan used traditional techniques, patterns, materials, and colors, she manipulated the elements of construction to

produce extraordinary quilts. Though Susan sewed appliqué quilts reminiscent of those favored by Methodist church groups on the East Coast, hers stand apart. Inspired by her prolific garden, McCord's appliquéd floral urns are whimsically overrun with plants of different species—fuschia, tulip, and daisy. Susan's urn quilts are surrounded by four different trailing vine borders.

Similarly, her pieced quilts may be traditional patterns, but they are set apart from their contemporaries in a number of ways. For example, Susan used a pattern called Ocean Waves, but

pieced it with exceptionally small scraps of calico, the hundreds of triangles surely taking countless hours to stitch together. Turkey Tracks is notable for its combination of dark brown piecing and pink lattice tracery. Both Ocean Waves and Turkey Tracks are actually pieced and appliquéd, for both are decorated with a sinuous green vine from which "grow" colorful buds and flowers. Her Hexagon Mosaic quilt is pieced in a pattern that echoes the shapes of the hundreds of bright scraps of hexagon-shaped cottons that form the quilt top. The resulting bedcover is vivid and dramatic.

The McCord contained "crazy" quilts (random shapes sewn "crazily" within self-contained blocks) appear strikingly unconventional to us. Susan's crazy blocks juxtapose color, texture and shape in unusual ways, rendering a rather modernistic "canvas." The quilt often referred to as "wheels" (see page 48) is actually a variation of a

Above and left: The vines in this most famous McCord quilt are dramatic in scale, breathtakingly "painted" with calico. While variations of the trailing vine are seen on a number of other McCord quilts, the theme is most significantly rendered here. The vine itself is of a previously-used calico, but the appliqué leaves and strip-pieced buds appear to be of unused scraps. There are two distinct stitching styles and two different colors of thread used to secure the scraps to the white cotton panel.

Right and below: The McCord Floral Urn quilt is reminiscent of "album" quilts, which are often composed of large appliqué floral or wreath blocks. This detail presents some of the design genius and exquisite workmanship for which the McCord quilts are famous. The urns contain a whimsical collection of flowers and strip-pieced leaves, with some flowers embellished with embroidery. Clusters of grapes are made from tiny circles of calico. The quilt's four different vine borders are shown here.

contained crazy quilt pattern called "fans," in which an arc or fan is sewn in the same position in each block. Instead, when Susan assembled her blocks, she scattered her fans in all four corners. When she joined the blocks, these fans converged, forming dynamic, colorful, wool flannel wheels.

Quilts are judged not only by composition, design and color, but by quality of workmanship. Susan McCord's piecing and quilting indicate that she was indeed a talented needleworker. The quilting that joins top, filler, and backing is unfailingly even, averaging about ten stitches per inch. Her patchwork quilts such as Ocean Waves (see page 44) and the two quilts formed of small hexagons (see pages 46 and 49) were laboriously pieced of hundreds of bits of cotton before Susan ever began quilting. While these bedcovers appear to have been constructed largely by a single hand, close examination indicates that Susan had assistance with at least some of the quilting and appliqué work. The scrap quilt called Diamond Field, her elegant Harrison Rose urn appliqué, and her well known vine appliqué quilt bear the

stitches of at least two different hands. Perhaps fellow Methodist church members or her two daughters shared her labors from time to time. Still, considering the intricacies of these ten quilts, it seems wondrous that even one quilt was completed!

Susan McCord's undisputed masterpiece is her "vine" quilt. Singled out as "unique and masterful" by the organizers of The Oakland Museum's 1981 exhibit "American Quilts: A Handmade Legacy," it is constructed of thirteen panels of appliqué vines. The execution is impressive, with over three hundred leaves and strip-pieced buds emanating from each vine. Few of the fabrics, with the exception of the green vines themselves, were taken from well-worn garments. Pencil marks, used to guide Susan's quilting needle, are still seen in spots along

the border. The colors remain fresh even after one hundred years. The fabrics, including the muslin ground, are crisp with sizing from the mills, indicating that the tiny scraps as well as the completed bedcover may never have been washed. We wonder whether Mrs. McCord saw this fine quilt as her masterpiece, or "best" quilt, and infrequently used it as a bedcover. Could it be that this appliqué quilt was constructed for aesthetic reasons only? The vine quilt is a piece of astonishing beauty, inspired by a passion for her garden, sewn from scraps of everyday materials, and quilted in snatches of time in the workaday world of a nineteenth-century homemaker.

Susan McCord's life and art are inextricably bound between the layers of the quilts featured in the gallery that follows. These bedcovers stand today as the extraordinary legacy of an otherwise little-known Indiana farmwife.

Susan McCord Quilt Gallery

On the gallery and project pages that follow, be inspired by Susan McCord's quilting geniu

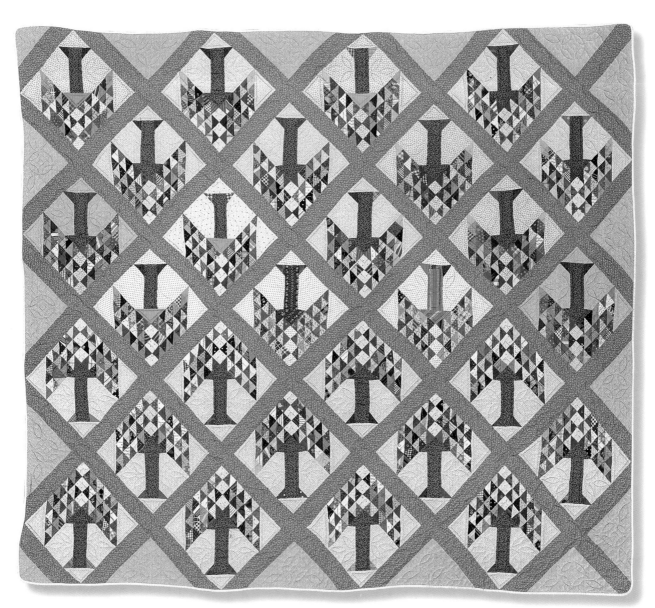

Pine Tree

The Pine Tree pattern top was pieced by Susan McCord but never finished. The family had it quilted several years ago and recently donated it to **The Henry Ford**. A close look reveals a few triangles of Susan McCord's characteristic pink calico. The sashing of purple calico is a delightful inclusion.

Object ID: 2004.17.1

Floral Urn

The two McCord Urn appliqué quilts (see page 60 for *Floral Urn Harrison Rose*) are representative of nine-block and four-block appliqué quilts, usually made predominately from red and green fabrics on a muslin or white background. These were popular "fancy" or "masterpiece" quilts in the mid-nineteenth century. Note Susan's inclusion of her "signature" pieced leaves in the blocks and along some vines.

Object ID: 72.140.2

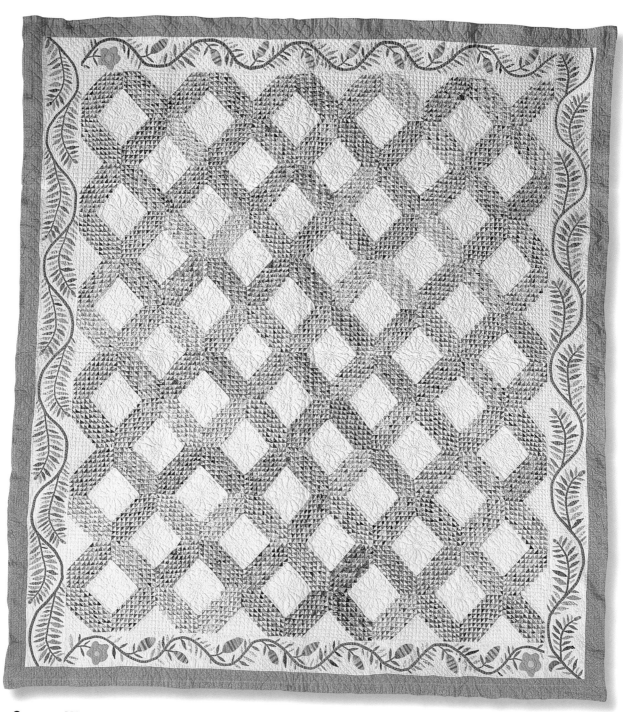

Ocean Waves

Mrs. McCord's pieced and appliqué quilts are of well-known, late-nineteenth century patterns. This bedcover is finely worked in hundreds of half-inch triangles of cotton. Once again, her unique vine and leaf motif is applied to the borders.

Object ID: 73.120.2

Feathered Star

The Prince's Feather, sometimes called Princess Feather, was a popular motif on quilts. By the time of the Civil War, quilters like Susan McCord produced appliqué pinwheeled stars using these feathers. Susan McCord's variation includes her dazzling strip-pieced leaves.

Object ID: 92.176.1

Turkey Tracks

This quilt is block-pieced in Turkey Tracks or Wandering Foot (a less popular name because, according to folklore, boys who slept beneath a Wandering Foot quilt would never settle down). It is combined with lattice sashing called Garden Maze and a single vine border, which suggests that the quilt was for a specific bed that had one long side against the wall. Thus, the single vine border would be clearly visible from the doorway.

Object ID: 73.120.6

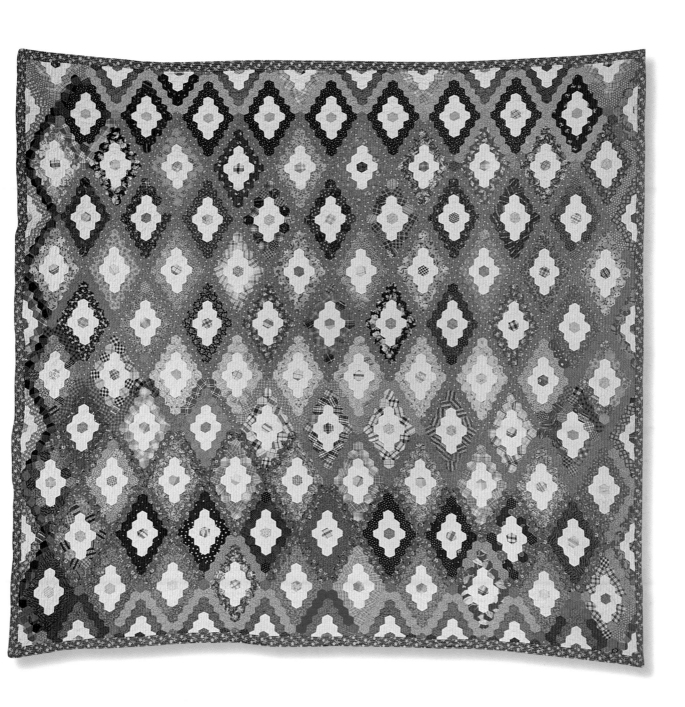

Diamond Field

This popular patchwork pattern employed many old clothing scraps. The evenly-faded quilt top and very thin batting indicate this quilt has seen much use and washing.

Object ID: 73.120.5

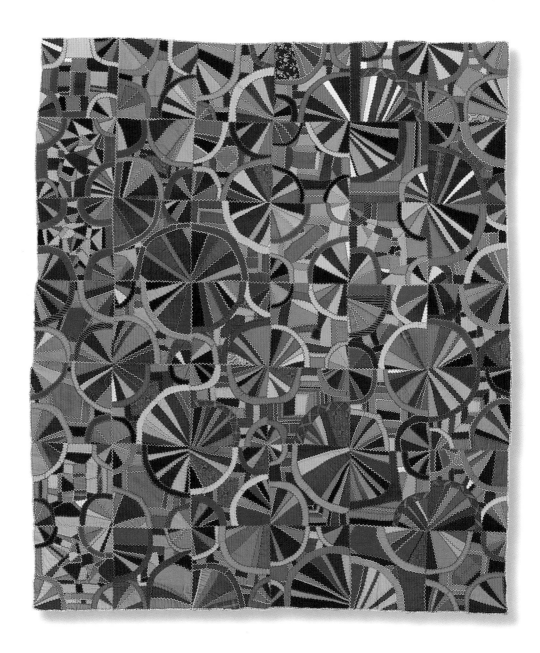

Fan Variation

This eye-dazzling textile is pieced of wool suiting and dress flannels in a variation of a crazy quilt pattern called Fan. This quilt was never finished; the blocks that contain the crazy piecing were only sewn together. It remains without backing.

Object ID: 73.120.7

Hexagon Mosaic

The Hexagon Mosaic pattern utilizes hundreds of scraps of dress remnants. Fabrics indicate that this is a later quilt that has not been frequently washed, in contrast with other McCord quilts.

Object ID: 76.120.4

Random with Embroidery

This is the only one of Susan McCord's crazy quilts to have been completed. It is an ambitious bedcover, indeed. Not only was it pieced, given a filler, and was tied together with a backing, but virtually every square is decorated with silk or crewel embroidery.

Object ID: 73.120.3

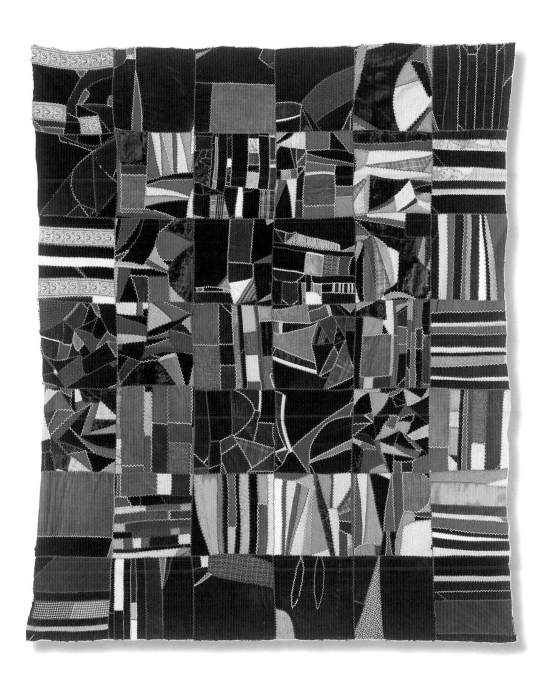

Random

Susan McCord never completed this crazy quilt, finishing only the pieced top. It is made of dress velvets and a few dress or millinery ribbons, enhanced with fancy stitching between the blocks.

Object ID: 73.120.8

Susan McCord
Quilts

The twelve quilts made by Indiana farmwife Susan McCord (1829–1909) that are in The Henry Ford collection are representative examples of typical midwestern quilting in terms of fabric use, color scheme, and technique. On another level, however, Mrs. McCord manipulated fabric, color and designs even on her quilts of traditional patterns, producing bedcovers far from ordinary. Here, and on the following pages, her most famous quilt—*McCord Vine*—and the *Floral Urn Harrison Rose* are offered as quilting projects.

Opposite: Susan McCord's magnificent appliqué *Vine Quilt* sits on the bedstead in the second-floor master bedroom of Harvey Firestone's boyhood home, from eastern Ohio. The furnishings date to circa 1880, just about the date of Susan McCord's Indiana quilt.

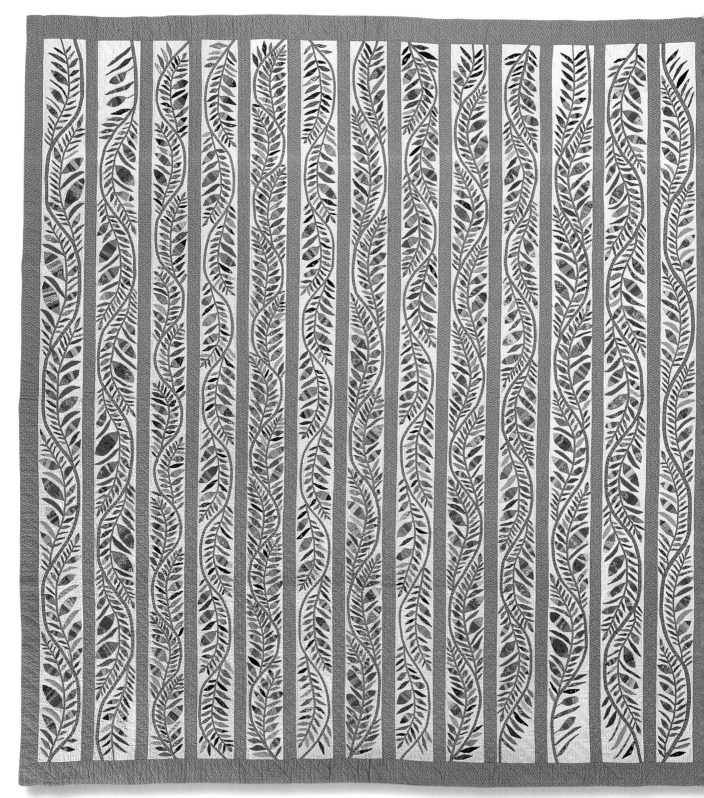

The opportunity to see this famous quilt in person was one of the highlights of our first trip to The Henry Ford. Strip piecing methods will speed up construction of the leaves somewhat, but this is a project to take along with you to sew in found moments. Work the leaves, panel by panel. ——*Marianne*

McCord Vine Quilt

A stunningly intricate display quilt, Susan McCord's Vine masterpiece is virtually an encyclopedia of the cotton calicos available in the mid-1800s. This quilt, the most famous McCord textile, is decorated with thirteen panels of Susan's sinuous vine. The leaves and buds, almost all cut from scraps of new material, are still crisp with sizing from the mill. Colors have not faded.

(*Note:* For the quilt projects, some of the dimensions and patterns may have been altered slightly to conform to today's cutting and piecing techniques.)

McCord Vine

Each panel of vine has more than 300 leaves and strip-pieced buds cut from scraps of many different florals, plaids, stripes and solids; the vines are a green printed cotton. The quilting is diamond or outline, nine to ten stitches to the inch. The back is plain muslin. The appliqué stitches show evidence of a second pair of hands.

Object ID: 72.140.1

McCord Vine

PROJECT RATING: INTERMEDIATE
Size: 80½" x 85"

Materials

4¾ yards cream solid for
 background
3 yards pink print for sashing,
 borders, and binding
3 yards green print for vines, stems,
 and leaves
20 fat quarters★ assorted pink, red,
 and burgundy prints for leaves
Paper-backed fusible web (optional)
7⅛ yards backing fabric
Queen-size quilt batting
★fat quarter = 18" x 20"

Cutting

Measurements include ¼" seam
allowances. Border strips are
exact length needed. You may
want to make them longer to
allow for piecing variations. Follow
manufacturer's instructions if using
fusible web.

From cream solid, cut:
- 2 (80½"-long) pieces. From pieces,
 cut 13 (5"-wide) **lengthwise** strips
 for appliqué backgrounds.

From pink print, cut:
- 1 (81"-long) piece. From piece, cut
 2 (3" x 81") **lengthwise** strips for
 top and bottom borders,
 2 (2½" x 80½") **lengthwise**
 strips for side borders, and
 12 (2" x 80½") **lengthwise**
 sashing strips.
- 9 (2¼"-wide) strips for binding.

From green print, cut:
- 1 (40"-long) piece. From piece,
 cut 1300" of 1⅛"-wide bias
 strips. Join strips; press strips in
 thirds for vines. From folded bias,
 cut 13 (100"-long) vines.
- 3 (9"-long) pieces. From pieces,
 cut 91 (⅝"-wide) bias strips
 for stems. Press strips in thirds
 for stems.
- 8 (1¼"-wide) strips. Cut strips in
 half to make 16 (1¼" x 20") strips
 for strip sets.
- 16 (1"-wide) strips. Cut strips in
 half to make 32 (1" x 20") strips
 for strip sets.

From fat quarters, cut:
- 148 strips in varying widths
 ranging from ¾"–1⅛" for Strip
 Sets A and B.
- 19 (1½"-wide) strips for Strip
 Set C.
- 1664 leaves in various sizes. (Cut
 leaves freehand. See diagrams on
 page 58 for examples of leaves.)

Strip Set Assembly

1. Referring to *Strip Set A Diagram*,
join 1 (1¼"-wide) green print strip
and 7 assorted red/pink/burgundy
print strips to complete Strip Set A.
Make 16 strip sets. From strip sets,
freehand cut 182 leaves.

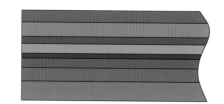

Strip Set A Diagram

2. Referring to *Strip Set B Diagram*,
join 1 (1"-wide) green print strip
and 3 assorted red/pink/burgundy
print strips to complete Strip Set B.
Make 12 strip sets. From strip sets,
freehand cut 273 leaves.

Strip Set B Diagram

3. Referring to *Strip Set C
Diagram*, join 1 (1"-wide) green
print strip and 1 (1½"-wide)
red/pink/burgundy print strip to
complete Strip Set C. Make 19 strip
sets. From strip sets, freehand cut
728 leaves.

Strip Set C Diagram

Quilt Assembly

1. Referring to *Quilt Top
Assembly Diagram*, lay out vines,
stems, and leaves on appliqué
background as shown. Appliqué
pieces to background. Make 13
appliqué strips.
2. Lay out appliqué strips and
sashing strips as shown in *Quilt
Top Assembly Diagram*. Join strips to
complete quilt center.
3. Add side borders to quilt. Add top
and bottom borders to quilt.

Finishing

1. Divide backing into 3 (2⅜-yard) pieces. Join panels lengthwise. Seams will run horizontally.

2. Layer backing, batting, and quilt top; baste. Quilt as desired. Quilt shown has echo quilting around the appliqué, diamonds in the sashing, and diagonal lines in the border.

3. Join 2¼"-wide pink print strips into 1 continuous piece for straight-grain French-fold binding. Add binding to quilt.

Quilt Top Assembly Diagram

Vine
Diagram

Join Vine
Top Here

Vine Bottom

Pieces are shown
actual size.
Add $3/16$" seam
allowance for
hand appliqué.

Vine Top

McCord Vine Quilt

The four different border designs epitomize Susan McCord's genius. She was so creative she couldn't stop at one idea. Make this quilt and win a blue ribbon at a national quilt show!

———Liz

Floral Urn
Harrison Rose Quilt

The large flower in the center of the urn is frequently seen on Hoosier quilts. Known as the Harrison Rose, it was named for the Indiana territory's first governor and ninth United States President, William Henry Harrison. Each edge is decorated with a different trailing vine.

(*Note:* For the quilt projects, some of the dimensions and patterns may have been altered slightly to conform to today's cutting and piecing techniques.)

oral Urn Harrison Rose

te cotton blocks are appliquéd
green urns and petaled flowers.
an McCord used three different
n prints for urns, vines, and
ge, and several pinks and reds
eaves and flowers. The quilting
ches are 10 to 12 per inch; the
cate quilting is mostly outline
small diamonds.

ect ID: 73.120.1

Floral Urn Harrison Rose

PROJECT RATING: INTERMEDIATE
Size: 78" x 82"
Blocks: 9 (22") Floral Urn blocks

Materials

6 yards cream solid for background, border, and binding

3 yards green print for appliqué and binding

1¾ yards red solid for appliqué and piping

¾ yard pink print for appliqué

½ yard yellow solid for appliqué

1 fat eighth★ orange solid for appliqué

Paper-backed fusible web (optional)

Green embroidery floss

Rug-weight acrylic yarn for piping

Zipper foot or piping foot for sewing maching

Clear monofilament thread

Glue stick

7⅛ yards backing fabric

Queen-size quilt batting

★fat eighth = 9" x 20"

Cutting

Patterns for appliqué are on pages 64–66. Follow manufacturer's instructions if using fusible web. Measurements include ¼" seam allowances. Border strips are exact length needed. You may want to make them longer to allow for piecing variations.

From cream solid, cut:

- 1 (68"-long) piece. From piece, cut 2 (8½" x 66½") **lengthwise** strips for top and bottom borders and 3 (22½") background squares.
- 1 (92"-long) piece. From piece, cut 2 (6½" x 78½") **lengthwise** strips for side borders and 4 (22½") background squares.
- 2 (22½"-wide) strips. From strips, cut 2 (22½") background squares.

From green print, cut:

- 1 (40"-long) piece. From piece, cut about 1240" of 1⅛"-wide bias strips. Join strips; press in thirds to make folded bias for stems. From folded bias, cut 75 (10"-long) stems and 17 (5"-long) stems. Remaining folded bias is for vine in border.
- 9 (2½"-wide) strips for binding.
- 9 Urns.
- 72 leaf 1.
- 18 Leaf 2.
- 27 Leaf 3.
- 27 Leaf 3 reversed.
- 42 Leaf 4.
- 18 Leaf 5.
- 9 Upper Feather.
- 9 Upper Feather reversed.
- 18 Flower 1 Small Center Circle.
- 9 Flower 2 Base.
- 24 Flower 5 Base.
- 9 Flower 6 Base.

From red solid, cut:

- 9 (1"-wide) strips for piping.
- 9 Lower Feather.
- 9 Lower Feather reversed.
- 63 Flower 1 Petal 1.
- 63 Flower 1 Petal 1 reversed.
- 18 Flower 1 Petal 2.
- 18 Flower 1 Petal 2 reversed.
- 9 Flower 2 Outer Flower.
- 9 Flower 3 Outer Flower.
- 9 Flower 3 Diamond.
- 18 Flower 4 Large Center Circle.
- 24 Flower 5 Bud.
- 18 Flower 6 Petal.
- 27 Flower 6 Circle.

From pink print, cut:

- 9 Flower 2 Inner Flower.
- 9 Flower 3 Inner Flower.
- 9 Flower 3 Large Center Circle.
- 26 Flower 4.
- 24 Flower 5 Accent.
- 24 Flower 7 Petal.

From yellow solid, cut:

- 18 Flower 1 Large Center Circle.
- 9 Flower 2 Center.
- 9 Flower 3 Outer Circle.
- 9 Flower 3 Small Center Circle.
- 18 Flower 4 Small Center Circle.
- 8 Flower 4 Large Center Circle.
- 24 Flower 5 Tip.
- 18 Flower 6 Petal.
- 24 Flower 7 Petal.

From orange solid, cut:

- 27 Urn Circles.

Block Assembly

1. Lay out feathers, leaves, stems, and flowers on block background as shown in *Block Diagram*. Appliqué pieces to background.

Block Diagram

2. Using 3 strands of green embroidery floss, stem stitch stems for leaves #1 and #2 to complete block. (See *Stem Stitch Diagram* on page 202.) Make 9 blocks.

Quilt Assembly

1. Referring to *Quilt Top Assembly Diagram*, lay out blocks as shown. Join into horizontal rows; join rows to complete quilt center.

2. Referring to *Quilt Top Assembly Diagram*, appliqué leaves, stems, vine, and flowers on top border. Add border to quilt center. Repeat for bottom and side borders.

Finishing

1. Divide backing into 3 (2⅜-yard) pieces. Join panels lengthwise. Seams will run horizontally.

2. Layer backing, batting, and quilt top; baste. Quilt as desired. Quilt shown was outline quilted around appliqué shapes and has a diagonal grid on the urns and background.

3. Join 2½"-wide cream strips into 1 continuous piece for straight-grain French-fold binding. Join 1"-wide red solid strips into 1 continuous piece for piping. See *Sew Easy: Binding with Piping* on page 135 for instructions to finish quilt with this detail. Add binding to quilt.

Quilt Top Assembly Diagram

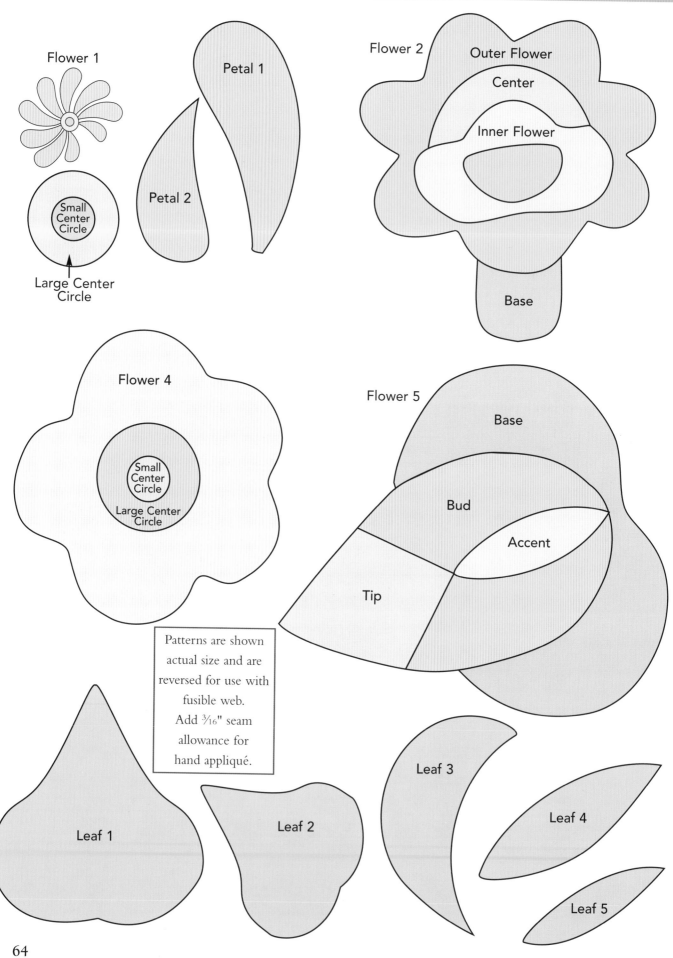

Flower 1

Petal 1

Petal 2

Small Center Circle

Large Center Circle

Flower 2

Outer Flower

Center

Inner Flower

Base

Flower 4

Small Center Circle

Large Center Circle

Flower 5

Base

Bud

Accent

Tip

Patterns are shown actual size and are reversed for use with fusible web. Add ³⁄₁₆" seam allowance for hand appliqué.

Leaf 1

Leaf 2

Leaf 3

Leaf 4

Leaf 5

64

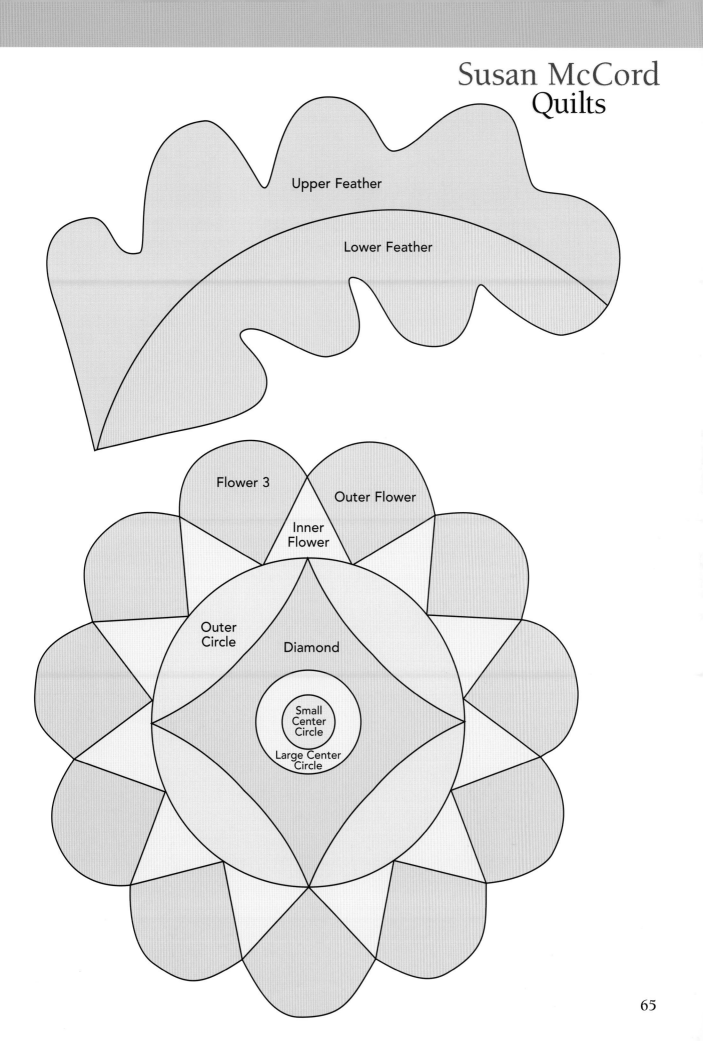

Upper Feather

Lower Feather

Flower 3

Outer Flower

Inner
Flower

Outer
Circle

Diamond

Small
Center
Circle

Large Center
Circle

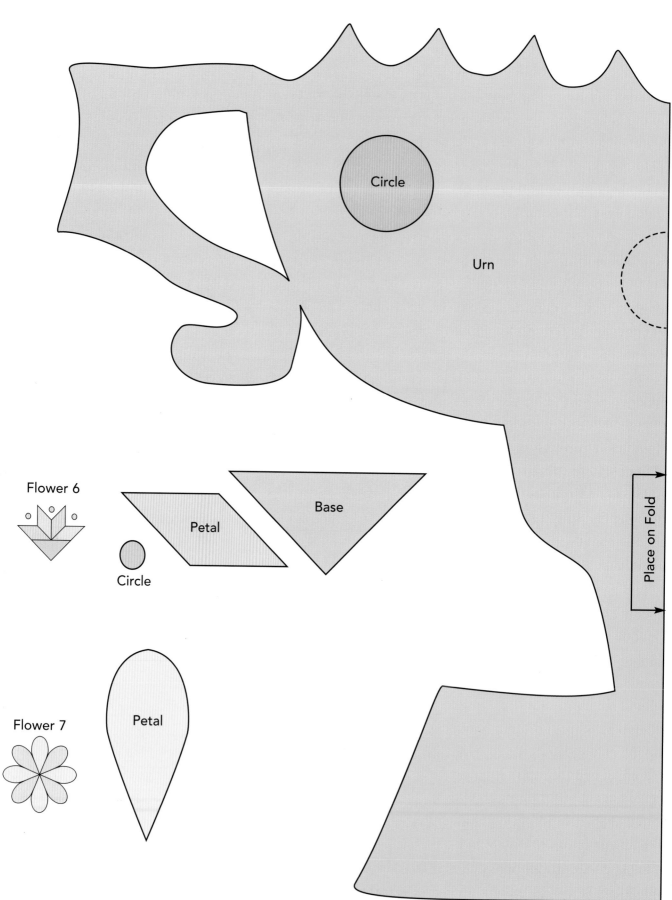

Circle

Urn

Place on Fold

Flower 6

Petal

Base

Circle

Flower 7

Petal

Floral Urn Harrison Rose Quilt

Red & White
Quilts

were a variation of two-color quilts made popular by the women's magazines of the early 1900s. Simple, geometric designs incorporated white and one other color—almost always red or blue.

A technique often referred to as Robbing Peter to Pay Paul was used for the *Four Hearts* quilt project that follows. Other classic patterns such as *Double Wedding Ring*, *Sunburst Medallion* and *Feathered Star* are also featured as quilting projects in this chapter.

Opposite: The Robbing Peter to Pay Paul pattern of this *Four Hearts* (circa 1870) quilt covers Bishop Milton Wright's bed in his Dayton, Ohio home. Books in this bedroom and the sitting room formed Orville and Wilbur Wright's (the Wright Brothers) personal library.

*I personally love the geometry of Robbing Peter to Pay Paul types of patterns.
As much as I enjoy print-fabric scrap quilts, I appreciate the simplicity of a
two-color quilt like this one.*

——Liz

Four Hearts Quilt

Robbing Peter to Pay Paul is not so much a pattern as it is a technique—one that is used with many different quilt patterns. In Robbing Peter to Pay Paul, geometric shapes are repeated in an overall pattern, in strongly contrasting colors, often red and white. The focus is not on individual blocks but on the overall balance of the design. In this quilt, four stylized hearts in a block form the scalloped edges of the adjacent square blocks.

(Note: For the quilt projects, some of the dimensions and patterns may have been altered slightly to conform to today's cutting and piecing techniques.)

Four Hearts

In this quilt from the late 1800s, pieced blocks of red and white cotton are set on the square. Each of the strip borders is 1½ inches wide. The quilting, in red and white threads, is diagonal in most of the quilt, with outline and echo in the quatrefoil shapes formed by pattern blocks. A traditional name for this kind of pattern is Robbing Peter to Pay Paul.

Object ID: 00.119.29

Four Hearts

PROJECT RATING: EASY

Size: 75" x 81½"

Blocks: 21 (11") Red Heart blocks and 21 (11") White Heart blocks

Materials

5¼ yards white solid for blocks, borders, and binding

4¼ yards red solid for blocks and border

5¼ yards backing fabric

Full-size quilt batting

Paper-backed fusible web (optional)

Cutting

Measurements include ¼" seam allowances. Border strips are exact length needed. You may want to make them longer to allow for piecing variations. Pattern for heart appliqué piece is on page 73. Follow manufacturer's instructions if using fusible web.

From white solid, cut:

• 7 (11½"-wide) strips. From strips, cut 21 (11½") background squares.

• 12 (2"-wide) strips. Piece strips to make 2 (2" x 77½") side inner borders, 1 (2" x 69½") bottom inner border, 2 (2" x 80½") side outer borders, and 1 (2" x 75½") bottom outer border.

• 9 (2¼"-wide) strips for binding.

• 84 heart appliqué pieces.

From red solid, cut:

• 7 (11½"-wide) strips. From strips, cut 21 (11½") background squares.

• 6 (2"-wide) strips. Piece strips to make 2 (2" x 79") side middle borders and 1 (2" x 72½") bottom middle border.

• 84 heart appliqué pieces.

Block Assembly

1. Appliqué 1 white heart piece to each corner of a red background square to complete 1 white Heart block *(White Heart Block Diagram).* Make 21 white Heart blocks.

White Heart Block Diagram

2. Appliqué 1 red heart piece to each corner of a white background square to complete 1 red Heart block *(Red Heart Block Diagram).* Make 21 red Heart blocks.

Red Heart Block Diagram

Quilt Assembly

1. Lay out blocks as shown in *Quilt Top Assembly Diagram.* Join into horizontal rows; join rows to complete quilt center.

2. Add white side inner borders to quilt center. Add white bottom inner border to quilt.

3. Repeat for red middle borders and white outer borders.

Finishing

1. Divide backing into 2 (2⅝-yard) pieces. Divide 1 piece in half lengthwise to make 2 narrow panels. Sew 1 narrow panel to each side of wider panel; press seam allowances toward narrow panels.

2. Layer backing, batting, and quilt top; baste. Quilt as desired. Quilt shown was quilted with diagonal lines in the block backgrounds and borders and with echo quilting in the hearts.

3. Join 2¼"-wide white strips into 1 continuous piece for straight-grain French-fold binding. Add binding to quilt.

Quilt Top Assembly Diagram

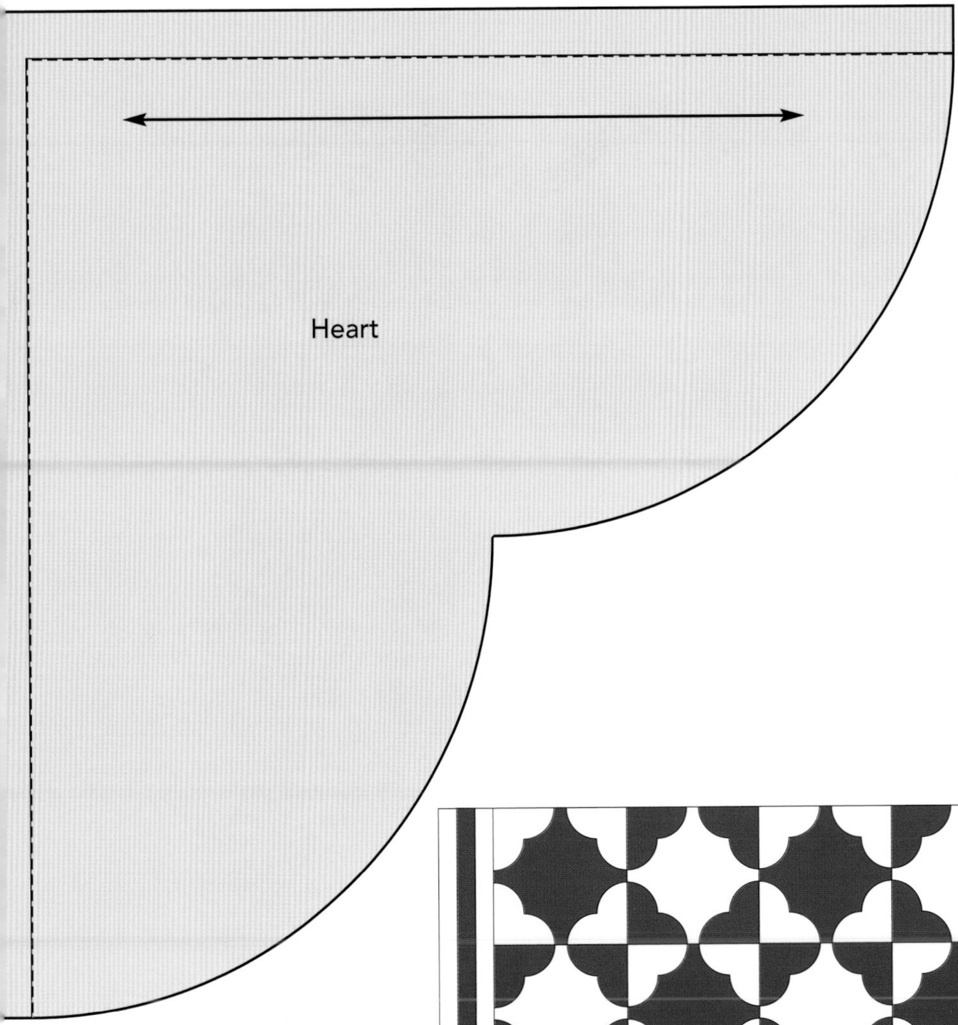

Heart

Curved edge is
shown finished size.
Add ³⁄₁₆" seam
allowance for
hand appliqué.

Four Hearts Quilt

There is something syncopated and "jazzy" about this quilt—I'd love to meet the lady who made it. Try using ten or twenty different red prints combined with a variety of shirting prints for the background.
                                                                    ——Marianne

Double Wedding Ring Quilt

This is a transitional quilt in its color and design, reflecting trends of the times just before and just after the quilt was made. Red-and-white quilts were popular from 1880 to 1920; Wedding Ring quilts became popular around 1920.

(*Note:* For the quilt projects, some of the dimensions and patterns may have been altered slightly to conform to today's cutting and piecing techniques.)

Double Wedding Ring

The top is pieced in Turkey red cotton and two different whites (possibly bleached and unbleached muslin). It has both hand and machine stitching, suggesting that the quilt top may have been worked on by different people over a period of time. The quilting is six to seven stitches per inch; it outlines the rings and is circular or floral in the white areas. The quilt was never washed and possibly never used.

Object ID: 73.205.14

Double Wedding Ring

PROJECT RATING: CHALLENGING
Size: 62¼" x 103¾"
Blocks: 15 (20¾"-diameter)
Wedding Ring blocks

Materials

8½ yards white solid for blocks and
  binding
2½ yards red solid for blocks
Template material
6¼ yards backing fabric
Queen-size quilt batting

Cutting

Patterns to make templates for
patchwork shapes are on pages
77–78. Measurements include ¼"
seam allowances.

From white solid, cut:

- 1 (34"-long) piece. From piece,
  cut 2¼"-wide bias strips. Join
  strips to make about 500" of bias
  for binding.
- 23 E pieces.
- 60 D pieces.
- 660 B pieces.
- 60 A pieces.
- 60 A reverse pieces.
- 4 (2⅛"-wide) strips. From strips,
  cut 60 (2⅛") C squares.

From red solid, cut:

- 660 B pieces.
- 60 A pieces.
- 60 A reverse pieces.
- 4 (2⅛"-wide) strips. From strips,
  cut 60 (2⅛") C squares.

Block Assembly

1. Lay out pieces as shown in *Ring
Segment Diagram*. Join 6 white and 5
red B pieces. Add 1 red A piece to
left end and 1 red A reverse piece to
right end to make 1 Ring Segment.
Make 2 Ring Segments. Add 1
white C square to each end of
1 segment.

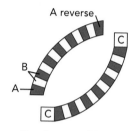

Ring Segment Diagram

2. Lay out Ring Segments and
1 white D piece as shown in *Melon
Unit Assembly Diagram*. Join pieces
to complete 1 white Melon Unit
(*Melon Unit Diagrams*). Make 2 white
Melon Units.

Melon Unit Assembly Diagram

3. Lay out pieces as shown in *Red
Melon Unit Diagram*. Repeat steps #1
and #2 to make 1 red Melon Unit.
Make 2 red Melon Units.

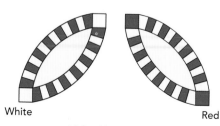

White   Red
Melon Unit Diagrams

4. Lay out 4 Melon Units and E
center piece as shown in *Block
Assembly Diagram*. Join pieces to
complete 1 Wedding Ring block
(*Block Diagram*). Make 15 blocks.

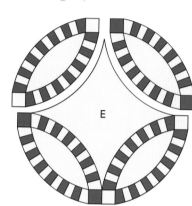

Block Assembly Diagram

Block Diagram

Quilt Assembly

1. Lay out blocks and E pieces
as shown in *Quilt Top Assembly
Diagram*.

2. Join blocks into horizontal rows,
adding E pieces between them.

3. Join rows to complete quilt top.

Finishing

1. Divide backing into 2 (3⅛-yard) pieces. Divide 1 piece in half lengthwise to make 2 narrow panels. Sew 1 narrow panel to each side of wider panel; press seam allowances toward narrow panels.

2. Layer backing, batting, and quilt top; baste. Quilt as desired. Quilt shown was outline quilted around the rings and in all the wedges and has a floral motif in each E piece.

3. Add binding to quilt.

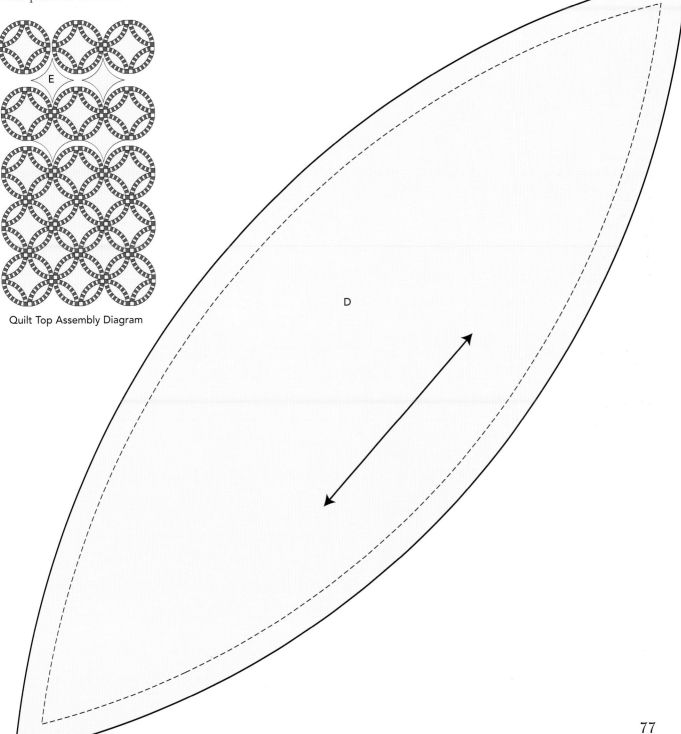

Quilt Top Assembly Diagram

D

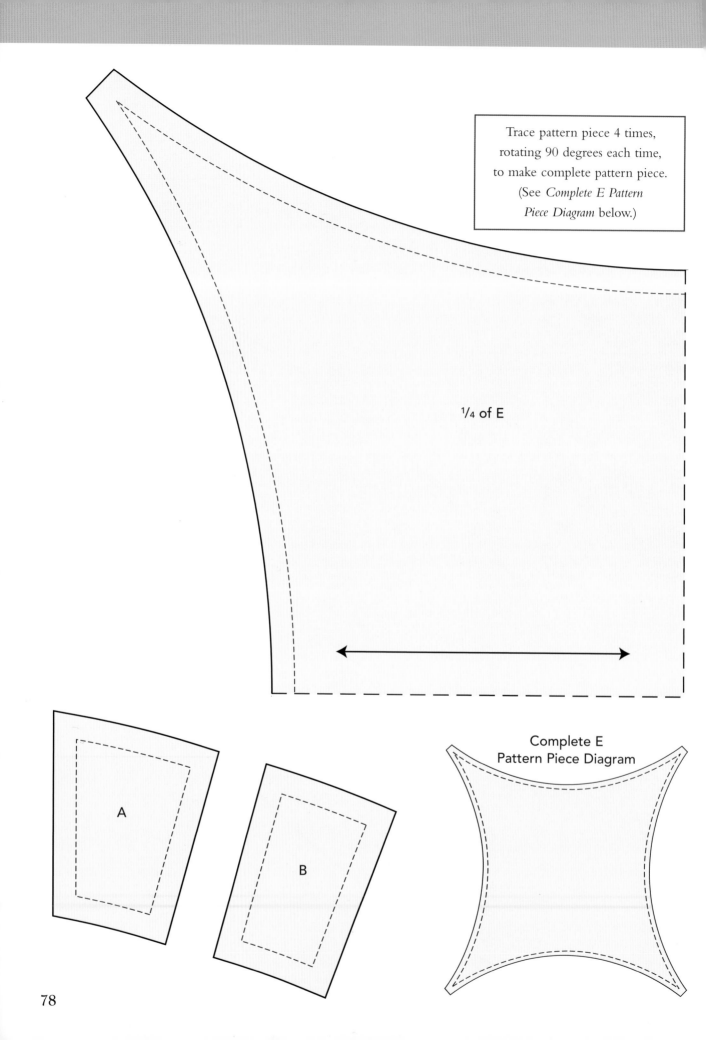

Trace pattern piece 4 times, rotating 90 degrees each time, to make complete pattern piece. (See *Complete E Pattern Piece Diagram* below.)

¹/₄ of E

A

B

Complete E
Pattern Piece Diagram

Double Wedding Ring Quilt

This medallion appears to be simply "made up" by its anonymous creator. For a square, king-size bed, buy extra fabric and make several more rows of red and white sawtooth triangles divided by white fabric spacers. ——*Liz*

Sunburst Medallion Quilt

Medallion quilts feature a large central block, usually appliquéd. In the earlier decades of American quiltmaking, medallion quilts were characteristically entirely appliquéd. From the late 1800s, the central medallion was usually surrounded by pieced designs. In this quilt, rows of Delectable Mountains and sawtooth borders create a frame for the focal point, the appliquéd thirteen-point Sunburst.

(*Note:* For the quilt projects, some of the dimensions and patterns may have been altered slightly to conform to today's cutting and piecing techniques.)

Sunburst Medallion

Possibly made in Canada around 1890, this cotton quilt has a Sunburst medallion in a square, set on point. The two rows of Delectable Mountains and the inner and outer sawtooth borders are pieced. The appliqué and some piecing are hand sewn; most of the quilt is machine sewn. The quilting is in white thread, in a diamond crosshatch.

Object ID: 34.206.15

Sunburst Medallion

PROJECT RATING: CHALLENGING
Size: 76" x 76"

Materials

4¾ yards white solid for patchwork
4 yards red solid for patchwork and
  binding
Template material
4¾ yards backing fabric
Full-size quilt batting

Cutting

Patterns to make templates for
patchwork shapes are on page 84.
Because there are so many pieces
which are similar in size, you may
want to label them as you cut.
Measurements include ¼" seam
allowances.

From white solid, cut:

• 1 (16½"-wide) strip. From strip,
  cut 1 (16½") center background
  square.
• 3 (15"-wide) strips. From strips, cut
  6 (15") squares. Cut squares in half
  diagonally to make 12 half-square
  G triangles.
• 2 (11⅞"-wide) strips. From
  strips, cut 6 (11⅞") squares.
  Cut squares in half diagonally
  in both directions to make 24
  quarter-square H triangles.
• 1 (5"-wide) strip. From strip, cut 2
  (5") squares. Cut squares in half
  diagonally in both directions to
  make 8 quarter-square K triangles.
• 12 (2⅞"-wide) strips. From strips,
  cut 148 (2⅞") squares. Cut squares
  in half diagonally to make 296
  half-square F triangles.
• 7 (2¾"-wide) strips. From strips,
  cut 96 (2¾") squares. Cut squares

in half diagonally to make 192
half-square J triangles.
• 3 (2½"-wide) strips. From strips,
  cut 4 (2½" x 4½") D rectangles
  and 28 (2½") E squares.
• 2 (2⅜"-wide) strips. From strips,
  cut 32 (2⅜") I squares.
• 13 B triangles.

From red solid, cut:

• 3 (11⅞"-wide) strips. From
  strips, cut 8 (11⅞") squares.
  Cut squares in half diagonally
  in both directions to make 32
  quarter-square H triangles.
• 1 (4½"-wide) strip. From strip, cut
  12 (2½" x 4½") D rectangles.
• 12 (2⅞"-wide) strips. From strips,
  cut 148 (2⅞") squares. Cut squares
  in half diagonally to make 296
  half-square F triangles.
• 8 (2¾"-wide) strips. From strips,
  cut 104 (2¾") squares. Cut squares
  in half diagonally to make 208
  half-square J triangles.
• 2 (2½"-wide) strips. From strips,
  cut 20 (2½") E squares.
• 2 (2⅜"-wide) strips. From strips,
  cut 24 (2⅜") I squares.
• 8 (2¼"-wide) strips for binding.
• 1 C circle.
• 13 A diamonds.

Center Block Assembly

1. Lay out 13 red A diamonds and
13 white B triangles as shown in
Sunburst Assembly Diagrams. Join 1
white B triangle to each diamond.
Join diamonds to make the
Sunburst. Appliqué Sunburst to
white background square *(Sunburst
Unit Diagram).* Turn under ¼" on
outer edge of C center circle and

appliqué atop Sunburst. Trim away
excess fabric from behind Sunburst.

Sunburst Assembly Diagrams

Sunburst Unit Diagram

2. Referring to *Flying Geese
Diagrams,* place 1 red E square atop
white D rectangle, right sides facing
Stitch diagonally from corner to
corner. Trim ¼" beyond stitching.
Press open to reveal triangle. Repeat
on opposite corner to complete 1
white Flying Geese Unit. Make 4
white Flying Geese Units.

Flying Geese Diagrams

3. Join 1 white F triangle and 1
red F triangle to make a
triangle-square. Make 296 F
triangle-squares.

4. Lay out F triangle-squares and
white Flying Geese Unit as shown
in *Border Diagram.* Join pieces to
complete 1 border. Make 4 borders.

Border Diagram

82

Join 1 border to each side of unburst as shown in *Center Block Assembly Diagram*. Add 1 white E square to each end of remaining 2 orders. Add borders to top and ottom to complete center block (*Center Block Diagram*).

Center Block Assembly Diagram

Center Block Diagram

Quilt Assembly

Referring to *Assembly Diagram 1,* oin white G triangles to center block. f necessary, trim to 28½" square.

Flying Geese Unit

Assembly Diagram 1

Referring to Step #2 in Center lock Assembly, make 12 red Flying

Geese Units using red D rectangles and white E squares.

3. Lay out F triangle-squares and 4 red Flying Geese Units as shown in *Assembly Diagram 1*. Join pieces to make 4 borders.

4. Add side borders to quilt center. Add top and bottom borders to quilt.

5. Join 1 red J triangle and 1 white J triangle to make a triangle-square. Make 192 J triangle-squares.

6. Referring to *Assembly Diagram 2,* lay out H triangles, J triangle-squares, I squares, and J and K triangles around quilt center. Join into units as shown; add units to quilt center.

Flying Geese Unit

Assembly Diagram 2

7. Add 1 G triangle to each corner.
8. Lay out F triangle-squares, red Flying Geese Units, and E squares as shown. Join pieces to make borders; add borders to quilt center.
9. Referring to *Assembly Diagram 3,* lay out H triangles, J triangle-squares, I squares, and J and K triangles around quilt center. Join

into units as shown; add units to quilt center.

Flying Geese Unit

Assembly Diagram 3

10. Add 1 G triangle to each corner.

11. Lay out F triangle-squares, red Flying Geese Units, and E squares as shown. Join pieces to make borders; add borders to quilt center.

Finishing

1. Divide backing into 2 (2⅜-yard) pieces. Divide 1 piece in half lengthwise to make 2 narrow panels. Sew 1 narrow panel to each side of wider panel; press seam allowances toward narrow panels.

2. Layer backing, batting, and quilt top; baste. Quilt as desired. Quilt shown was quilted with an allover diamond grid.

3. Join 2¼"-wide red strips into 1 continuous piece for straight-grain French-fold binding. Add binding to quilt.

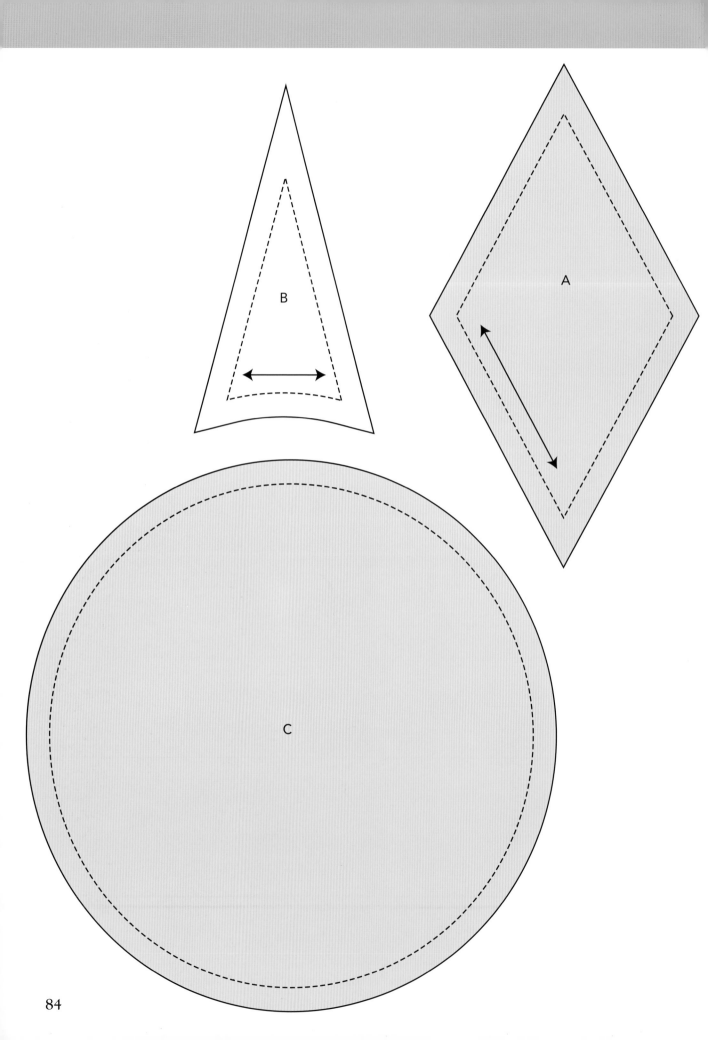

Sunburst Medallion Quilt

Feathered star patterns are not for the faint-hearted patchworker. The tiny half-square triangles that edge the stars make them vibrate visually. Put your finest quilting, whether by hand or machine, in the open white areas.

——*Marianne*

Feathered Star Quilt

Stars became a popular quilt motif in the second quarter of the 1800s. Popular eight-pointed stars were the Star of Bethlehem and the LeMoyne Star. The Variable Star and the Ohio Star are both built around a square. Adding a sawtooth border to any star is what makes it feathered. The Feathered Star in this red-and-white gem is a Variable Star.

(*Note:* For the quilt projects, some of the dimensions and patterns may have been altered slightly to conform to today's cutting and piecing techniques.)

Feathered Star

The 16 pattern blocks are pieced of white cotton and red cotton with roller-printed dots. There is an ½"-wide white border. The narrow sawtooth borders are pieced. The quilting, 8 stitches to the inch, is diagonal in the stars, crosshatch in the white areas, cable in the strip border, and straight line in the pieced borders. One corner has a handwritten signature in ink, "Mrs. T. Hall." Mrs. Hall probably finished her quilt around 1890.

Object ID: 29.495.51

Feathered Star

PROJECT RATING: CHALLENGING
Size: 88" x 88"

Materials

8 yards white solid for patchwork
  and binding
4 yards red solid for patchwork
Tracing paper
8¼ yards backing fabric
Queen-size quilt batting

Cutting

Patterns for foundation piecing
Units 1 and 2 are on page 91.
Because there are so many pieces
which are similar in size, you may
want to label them as you cut.
Measurements include ¼" seam
allowances. Border strips are exact
length needed. You may want to
make them longer to allow for
piecing variations.

From white solid, cut:
- 1 (86"-long) piece. From piece,
  cut 4 (8¾"-wide) **lengthwise**
  strips. From strips,
  cut 2 (8¾" x 85¾") top and
  bottom middle borders and 2
  (8¾" x 69¼") side middle borders.
- 1 (9⅞"-wide) strip. From strip, cut
  4 (9⅞") squares. Cut squares in
  half diagonally in both directions
  to make 16 E setting triangles.
- 3 (8½"-wide) strips. From strips,
  cut 9 (8½") H squares.
- 4 (6⅝"-wide) strips. From strips,
  cut 24 (6⅝") D squares.
- 4 (4½"-wide) strips. From strips,
  cut 12 (4½" x 8½") G rectangles
  and 4 (4½") F squares.

- 8 (2¼"-wide) strips. From strips,
  cut 126 (2¼") squares. Cut squares
  in half diagonally to make 252
  half-square J triangles.
- 9 (2¼"-wide) strips for binding.
- 6 (2⅛"-wide) strips. From strips,
  cut 108 (2⅛") squares. Cut squares
  in half diagonally to make 216
  half-square I triangles.
- 13 (1⅞"-wide) strips. From strips,
  cut 256 (1⅞") squares. Cut squares
  in half diagonally to make 512
  half-square A triangles.

From red solid, cut:
- 4 (7⅞"-wide) strips. From strips,
  cut 16 (7⅞") C squares.
- 8 (2¼"-wide) strips. From strips,
  cut 126 (2¼") squares. Cut squares
  in half diagonally to make 252
  half-square J triangles.
- 6 (2⅛"-wide) strips. From strips,
  cut 108 (2⅛") squares. Cut squares
  in half diagonally to make 216
  half-square I triangles.
- 10 (1⅞"-wide) strips. From strips,
  cut 192 (1⅞") squares. Cut squares
  in half diagonally to make 384
  half-square A triangles.
- 3 (1½"-wide) strips. From strips,
  cut 64 (1½") B squares.

Star Assembly

1. Trace Unit 1 foundation piecing
pattern on page 91. Foundation
piece unit in numerical order.
(See *Sew Easy: Paper Foundation
Piecing* on page 93.) Pieces #1, #3,
#5, #7, #9, and #11 are red, and
remaining pieces are white. Make 64
Unit 1 sections.

2. In the same manner, make 64
Unit 2 sections.

3. Join 1 white A triangle and 1 red
A triangle to make a triangle-square.
Make 24 A triangle-squares.

4. Lay out 3 A triangle-squares
and 1 white A triangle as shown
in *Unit 3 Diagram*. Join pieces to
complete 1 Unit 3. Make 4 of
Unit 3.

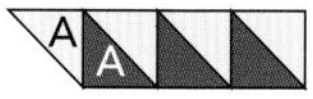

Unit 3 Diagram

5. Lay out 3 A triangle-squares, 1
white A triangle, and 1 red B square
as shown in *Unit 4 Diagram*. Join
pieces to complete 1 Unit 4. Make 4
of Unit 4.

Unit 4 Diagram

6. Lay out 1 red C square and Units
1–4 as shown in *Star Assembly
Diagram*. Join into horizontal rows;
join rows to complete 1 Feathered
Star *(Star Diagram)*. Make 16
Feathered Stars.

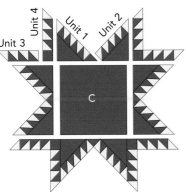

Star Assembly Diagram

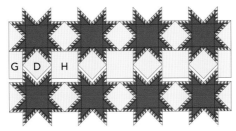

Star Diagram

Quilt Assembly

1. Referring to *Quilt Top Assembly Diagram*, lay out Feathered Stars in 4 horizontal rows with 4 stars in each row.

2. Join 4 Feathered Stars by setting in 1 E triangle at each end of row and 3 D squares between stars as shown in *Star Row Diagram*. Make 4 Star Rows.

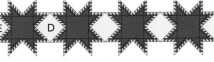

Star Row Diagram

3. Join rows by setting in 1 G rectangle at each end of row and 4 D squares and 3 H squares between stars as shown in *Row Joining Diagram*.

4. Set in F squares, E triangles, and G rectangles around perimeter of quilt to complete quilt center.

Row Joining Diagram

Border Assembly

1. Join 1 white I triangle and 1 red I triangle to make a triangle-square. Make 216 I triangle-squares.

2. Join 53 I triangle-squares as shown in *Quilt Top Assembly Diagram* to make side inner border. Repeat for other side border. Join 55 I triangle-squares to make top inner border. Repeat for bottom inner border.

3. Add side inner borders to quilt center. Add top and bottom inner borders to quilt.

4. Add side middle borders to quilt center. Add top and bottom middle borders to quilt.

5. Join 1 white J triangle and 1 red J triangle to make a triangle-square. Make 252 J triangle-squares.

6. Join 62 J triangle-squares as shown in *Quilt Top Assembly Diagram* to make side outer border. Repeat for other side border. Join 64 J triangle-squares to make top outer border. Repeat for bottom outer border.

7. Add side outer borders to quilt center. Add top and bottom outer borders to quilt.

Finishing

1. Divide backing into 3 (2¾-yard) pieces. Join panels lengthwise. Seams will run horizontally.

2. Layer backing, batting, and quilt top; baste. Quilt as desired. Quilt shown was quilted with an allover diagonal grid in the center, with straight lines parallel to edge of quilt in triangle borders, and with a cable design in the white middle border.

3. Join 2¼"-wide white strips into 1 continuous piece for straight-grain French-fold binding. Add binding to quilt.

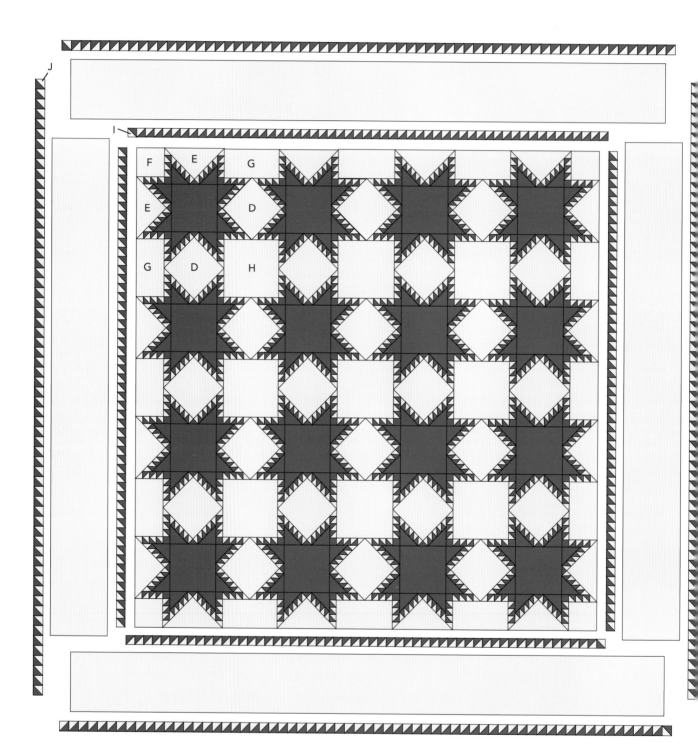

Quilt Top Assembly Diagram

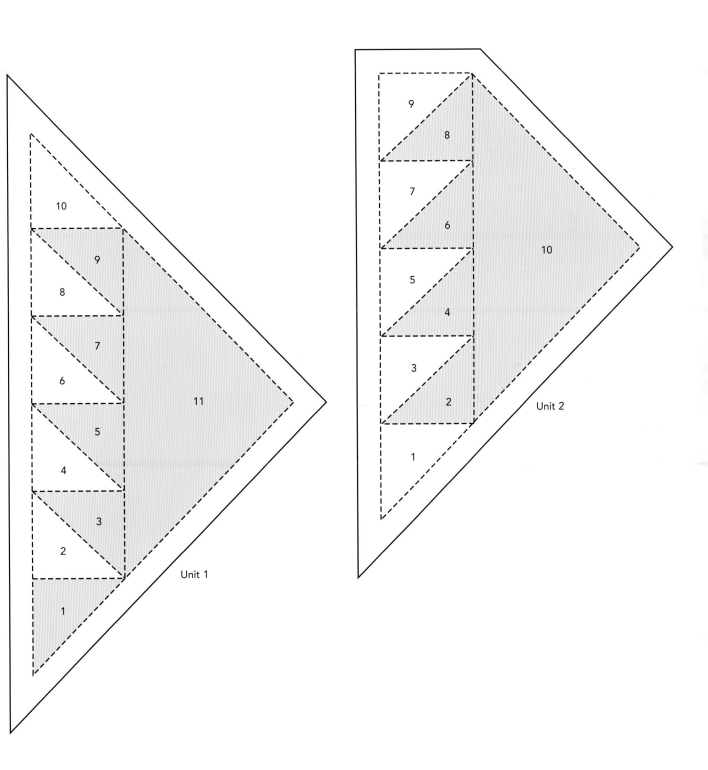

Feathered Star Quilt

Paper Foundation Piecing

Paper foundation piecing is ideal for small, intricate designs or designs with odd angles and sizes of pieces. Use this method for the units in the *Feathered Star* quilt on page 86.

Using ruler and pencil, trace the outline of all shapes and the outer edge of the foundation pattern onto tracing paper. Number the pieces to indicate the stitching order. Using fabric pieces that are larger than the numbered areas, place fabrics for #1 and #2 right sides together. Position paper pattern atop fabrics with printed side of paper facing you *(Photo A)*. Make sure the fabric for #1 is under that area and that edges of fabrics extend ¼" beyond stitching line between the two sections.

2. Using a short machine stitch so papers will tear off easily later, sew on stitching line between the two areas, extending stitching into seam allowances at ends of seams.

3. Open out pieces and press or finger press the seam *(Photo B)*. The right sides of the fabric pieces will be facing out on the back side of the paper pattern.

4. Flip the work over and fold back paper pattern on sewn line. Trim seam allowance to ¼", being careful not to cut paper pattern *(Photo C)*.

5. Continue to add pieces in numerical order until pattern is covered. Use rotary cutter and ruler to trim excess paper and fabric along outer pattern lines *(Photo D)*.

6. Join pieced sections to complete block *(Photo E)*.

7. Carefully tear off foundation paper.

B

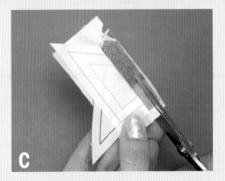

C

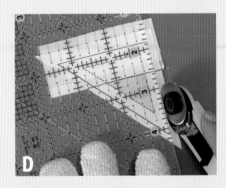

D

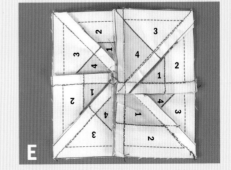

E

A

Sew Smart™

Instead of tracing paper, try one of the new water-soluble paper products. Instead of tearing off the paper after sewing, just moisten, and the paper disappears! —Liz

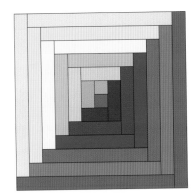

Log Cabin Quilts

Log Cabin Quilts have been a long-time favorite, popular since the mid-1800's. Successively longer strips of fabric are sewn clockwise or counter-clockwise around a center square as if the quilter is building a cabin of logs. The blocks can be assembled into many different arrangements such as Barn Raising, Straight Furrow, Courthouse Steps and zigzag or Streak of Lightning. These, and other well-known Log Cabin patterns are offered as projects on the following pages.

Opposite: This Log Cabin quilt sits outside the McGuffey Schoolhouse, built by Henry Ford in 1934. William Holmes McGuffey carefully chose the textbook entries for his McGuffey readers based on both instructional and moralistic content.

Build Your Best Log Cabin Quilt

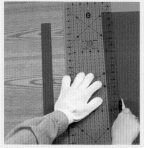

1. Select a block style—Traditional or Courthouse Steps Log Cabin.

2. Choose desired block size from the chart.

3. Sort scrap fabrics into lights and darks.

4. Let the appropriate chart be your guide for cutting strip widths and lengths.

5. Make blocks by adding strips around center square in numerical order.

6. Choose a setting for your blocks.

Traditional

Build this block by adding strips around a center square, dark on one side and light on the other. Chart on page 97.

Courthouse Steps

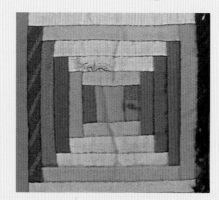

Build this block by adding pairs of light, then dark strips to opposite sides of the center square. Chart on page 99.

Log Cabin History

- Log Cabin quilts were a big fad in the 1860s and 70s, when both the pattern and technique were new.

- Log Cabin quilts first gained popularity after the Civil War, probably as a tribute to President Lincoln.

- Nineteenth century Log Cabin quilts were pieced on a foundation. Narrow strips of wool or cotton were laid atop a muslin (or paper) square, stitched down, and then pressed to one side in a technique called "press piecing."

- Because of their extra layer, Log Cabin quilts pieced on a foundation were often tied rather than quilted.

- Folklore says a red center square represents the log cabin's hearth, a yellow square, the lighted window.

Barn Raising

Straight Furrow

Traditional Log Cabin

The most common Log Cabin blocks build from the center out with strips added around the center square in either clockwise, as in the block at right, or counter-clockwise order.

Often, the blocks are shaded diagonally so half the block is light and the other dark. Shading in this manner allows for many setting options. The diagrams on this page and on page 98 illustrate just a few of the many options for setting these blocks.

TRADITIONAL LOG CABIN BLOCK CHART

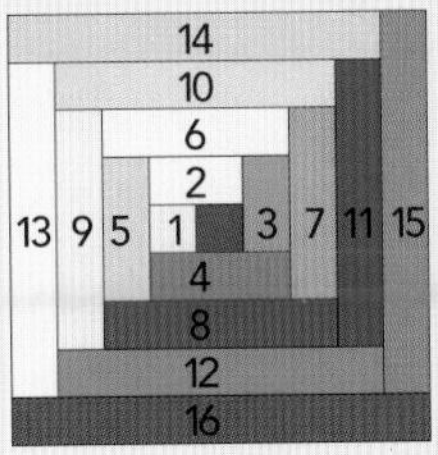

		BLOCK SIZE	4½"	6¾"	9"	11¼"	13½"
		CUT STRIP WIDTH	1"	1¼"	1½"	1¾"	2"
		SIZE FOR CENTER	1"	1¼"	1½"	1¾"	2"
LENGTHS TO CUT LIGHT STRIPS		#1	1"	1¼"	1½"	1¾"	2"
		#2	1½"	2"	2½"	3"	3½"
		#5	2"	2¾"	3½"	4½"	5"
		#6	2½"	3½"	4½"	5½"	6½"
		#9	3"	4¼"	5½"	6¾"	8"
		#10	3½"	5"	6½"	8"	9½"
		#13	4"	5¾"	7½"	9¼"	11"
		#14	4½"	6½"	8½"	10½"	12½"
LENGTHS TO CUT DARK STRIPS		#3	1½"	2"	2½"	3"	3½"
		#4	2"	2¾"	3½"	4¼"	5"
		#7	2½"	3½"	4½"	5½"	6½"
		#8	3"	4¼"	5½"	6¾"	8"
		#11	3½"	5"	6½"	8"	9½"
		#12	4"	5¾"	7½"	9¼"	11"
		#15	4½"	6½"	8½"	10½"	12½"
		#16	5"	7¼"	9½"	11¾"	14"

Lights and Darks

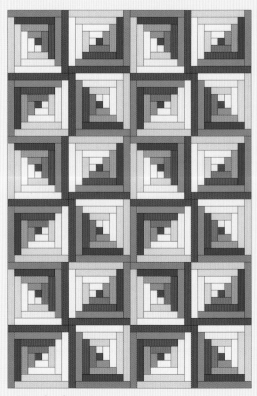

Pinwheels

Zigzag

Dirty Windows

Courthouse Steps Log Cabin

Courthouse Steps Log Cabin blocks are either shaded with two opposite sides of light fabrics and two of darker fabrics or made with four distinct colors, one for each side. With either shading method, strips are first added to two opposite sides of the center square and then to the remaining two sides.

COURTHOUSE STEPS LOG CABIN BLOCK CHART

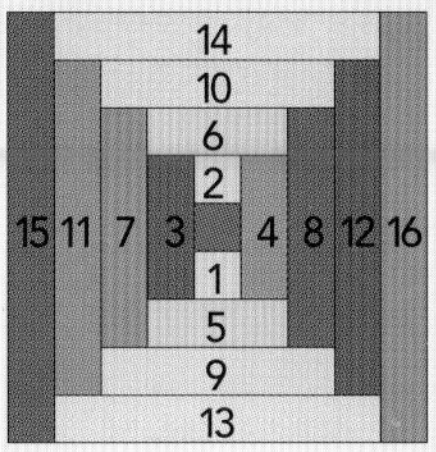

		BLOCK SIZE	4½"	6¾"	9"	11¼"	13½"
		CUT STRIP WIDTH	1"	1¼"	1½"	1¾"	2"
		SIZE FOR CENTER	1"	1¼"	1½"	1¾"	2"
LENGTHS TO CUT	LIGHT STRIPS	#1 & #2	1"	1¼"	1½"	1¾"	2"
		#5 & #6	2"	2¾"	3½"	4½"	5"
		#9 & #10	3"	4¼"	5½"	6¾"	8"
		#13 & #14	4"	5¾"	7½"	9¼"	11"
	DARK STRIPS	#3 & #4	2"	2¾"	3½"	4¼"	5"
		#7 & #8	3"	4¼"	5½"	6¾"	8"
		#11 & #12	4"	5¾"	7½"	9¼"	11"
		#15 & #16	5"	7¼"	9½"	11¾"	14"

Chimneys and Cornerstones Courthouse Steps Log Cabin

Chimneys and Cornerstones Courthouse Steps Log Cabin is a variation of the basic block with contrasting squares added at the corners where light and dark strips meet. The contrasting corner squares create diagonal grids when blocks are set together.

CHIMNEYS & CORNERSTONES COURTHOUSE STEPS LOG CABIN BLOCK CHART

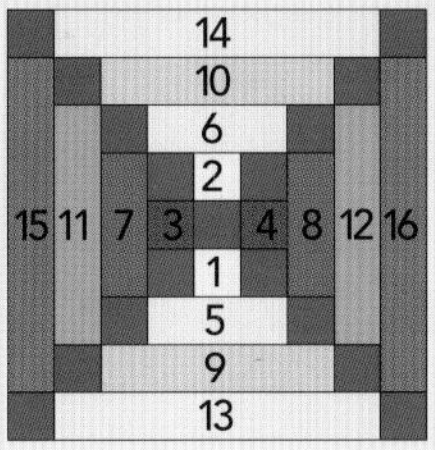

		BLOCK SIZE	4½"	6¾"	9"	11¼"	13½"
		CUT STRIP WIDTH	1"	1¼"	1½"	1¾"	2"
		SIZE FOR CENTER	1"	1¼"	1½"	1¾"	2"
LENGTHS TO CUT	LIGHT STRIPS	#1 & #2	1"	1¼"	1½"	1¾"	2"
		#5 & #6	2"	2¾"	3½"	4½"	5"
		#9 & #10	3"	4¼"	5½"	6¾"	8"
		#13 & #14	4"	5¾"	7½"	9¼"	11"
	DARK STRIPS	#3 & #4	1"	1¼"	1½"	1¾"	2"
		#7 & #8	2"	2¾"	3½"	4¼"	5"
		#11 & #12	3"	4¼"	5½"	6¾"	8"
		#15 & #16	4"	5¾"	7½"	9¼"	11"

*Log Cabins epitomize all that is wonderful about American quiltmaking—
economy in terms of fabric use, incredible design impact, and patterns named
for actual everyday historical events like neighbors working together to build
a barn in a day.*
                                                                ——*Liz*

Barn Raising Variation Quilt

Many Log Cabin quilts were not quilted. Instead, the quilt top, batting and backing were tied together with string or yarn at the corners or in the centers of the blocks. The quilt could then be disassembled for laundering, a health measure strongly advised by women's magazines of the day. Quilts made this way were referred to as "comforts," "comforters," or "comfortables."

(*Note:* For the quilt projects, some of the dimensions and patterns may have been altered slightly to conform to today's cutting and piecing techniques.)

Barn Raising Variation

Mary Anne Griffin McConnell of Upstate New York made this Log Cabin quilt for her first son, Silas. The two layers are tacked together, rather than quilted, at the corners where the blocks meet. The quilt is probably foundation pieced, with mostly solid colors of wool, cotton, and silk. The backing is two checked cottons, machine sewn.

Object ID: 81.17.1

Barn Raising Variation

PROJECT RATING: EASY
Size: 87¾" x 97½"
Blocks: 90 (9¾") Log Cabin blocks

Materials

30 fat quarters★ assorted dark prints for blocks
30 fat quarters★ assorted light prints for blocks
1 fat eighth★★ red solid for block centers
¾ yard brown solid for binding
7⅞ yards backing fabric
Queen-size quilt batting
★fat quarter = 18" x 20"
★★fat eighth = 9" x 20"

Cutting

Because there are so many pieces which are similar in size, you may want to label them as you cut. Measurements include ¼" seam allowances.

From each dark and light fat quarter, cut:

• 12 (1¼"-wide) strips. From strips, cut 3 sets of logs as listed in *Cutting Chart for 1 Log Cabin Block.*

From red solid, cut:

• 6 (1¼"-wide) strips. From strips, cut 90 (1¼") center squares.

From brown solid, cut:

• 10 (2¼"-wide) strips for binding.

Block Assembly

1. Lay out pieces as shown in *Log Cabin Block Diagram.*

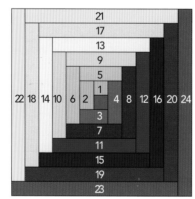

Log Cabin Block Diagram

2. Join strips in numerical order to complete 1 Log Cabin block. Make 90 Log Cabin blocks.

Quilt Assembly

1. Lay out blocks as shown in *Quilt Top Assembly Diagram.*
2. Join blocks into horizontal rows; join rows to complete quilt top.

Finishing

1. Divide backing into 3 (2⅝-yard) pieces. Join pieces to make quilt back. Seams will run horizontally.
2. Layer backing, batting, and quilt top; baste. Quilt as desired. Quilt shown is tied.
3. Join 2¼"-wide brown strips into 1 continuous piece for straight-grain French-fold binding. Add binding to quilt.

Quilt Top Assembly Diagram

Cutting Chart for 1 Log Cabin Block
CUT ALL STRIPS 1¼" WIDE

DARK STRIPS	LIGHT STRIPS	STRIP LENGTH
#24		10¼"
#23	#22	9½"
#20	#21	8¾"
#19	#18	8"
#16	#17	7¼"
#15	#14	6½"
#12	#13	5¾"
#11	#10	5"
#8	#9	4¼"
#7	#6	3½"
#4	#5	2¾"
#3	#2	2"
	#1	1¼"

Barn Raising Variation Quilt

When we started making quilts in the mid 1970s, there weren't enough different 100 percent cotton print fabrics available to even begin to make a fabulous quilt like this one which was created in the nineteenth-century heyday of American print cloth manufacture.

——*Marianne*

Straight Furrow Quilt

Turning alternate blocks so their dark halves come together forms the shading that resembles plowed fields with straight furrows—a familiar part of farm life for many nineteenth-century quilters. The quilt's roller-printed cotton backing, with its paisley challis prints in strong and beautiful colors, suggests the quilt was made in Pennsylvania.

(*Note:* For the quilt projects, some of the dimensions and patterns may have been altered slightly to conform to today's cutting and piecing techniques.)

Straight Furrow

Probably made in Pennsylvania during the 1870s or 80s, this dramatic hand-sewn quilt has a red wool "chimney" square centered in each of the 99 pattern blocks. It is foundation pieced of brocaded and printed patterns, including some silks. The quilting consists of square outline in the blocks and diagonal lines in the borders, five to six stitches to the inch.

Object ID: 74.128.6

Straight Furrow

PROJECT RATING: EASY
Size: 73½" x 87½"
Blocks: 99 (7½") Log Cabin blocks

Materials

50 fat eighths★ assorted dark prints
for blocks
33 fat eighths★ assorted light prints
for blocks
⅜ yard red solid for block centers
⅜ yard light green print
for border
½ yard brown print for border
¾ yard tan print for binding
5¼ yards backing fabric
Full-size quilt batting
★fat eighth = 9" x 20"

Cutting

Because there are so many
pieces which are similar in size,
you may want to label them as
you cut. Measurements include ¼"
seam allowances.

From each dark fat eighth, cut:
• 6 (1¼"-wide) strips. From strips,
cut 2 sets of logs as listed in
*Cutting Chart for 1 Log Cabin
Block.*

From each light fat eighth, cut:
• 6 (1¼"-wide) strips. From strips,
cut 3 sets of logs as listed in
*Cutting Chart for 1 Log Cabin
Block.*

From red solid, cut:
• 5 (2"-wide) strips. From strips, cut
99 (2") center squares.

From light green print, cut:
• 5 (3½"-wide) strips. Piece strips to
make 2 (3½" x 83") side borders.

From brown print, cut:
• 4 (3"-wide) strips. Piece strips to
make 2 (3" x 74") top and bottom
borders.

From tan print, cut:
• 9 (2¼"-wide) strips for binding.

Cutting Chart for 1 Log Cabin Block
CUT ALL STRIPS 1¼" WIDE

DARK STRIPS	LIGHT STRIPS	STRIP LENGTH
#16		8"
#15	#14	7¼"
#12	#13	6½"
#11	#10	5¾"
#8	#9	5"
#7	#6	4¼"
#4	#5	3½"
#3	#2	2¾"
	#1	2"

Block Assembly

1. Lay out pieces as shown in *Log
Cabin Block Diagram.*

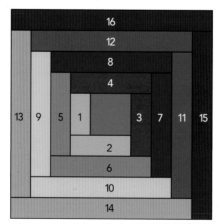

Log Cabin Block Diagram

2. Join strips in numerical order to
complete 1 Log Cabin block. Make
99 Log Cabin blocks.

Quilt Assembly

1. Lay out blocks as shown in *Quilt
Top Assembly Diagram.*
2. Join blocks into horizontal rows;
join rows to complete quilt center.
3. Add light green side borders
to quilt center. Add brown print
borders to top and bottom of quilt.

Finishing

1. Divide backing into 2 (2⅝-yard)
pieces. Divide 1 piece in half
lengthwise to make 2 narrow panels
Sew 1 narrow panel to each side of
wider panel; press seam allowances
toward narrow panels.
2. Layer backing, batting, and quilt
top; baste. Quilt as desired. Quilt
shown was quilted in the ditch
between blocks and with diagonal
lines in the border.
3. Join 2¼"-wide tan print strips
into 1 continuous piece for straight-
grain French-fold binding. Add
binding to quilt.

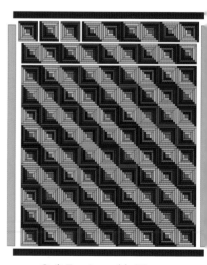

Quilt Top Assembly Diagram

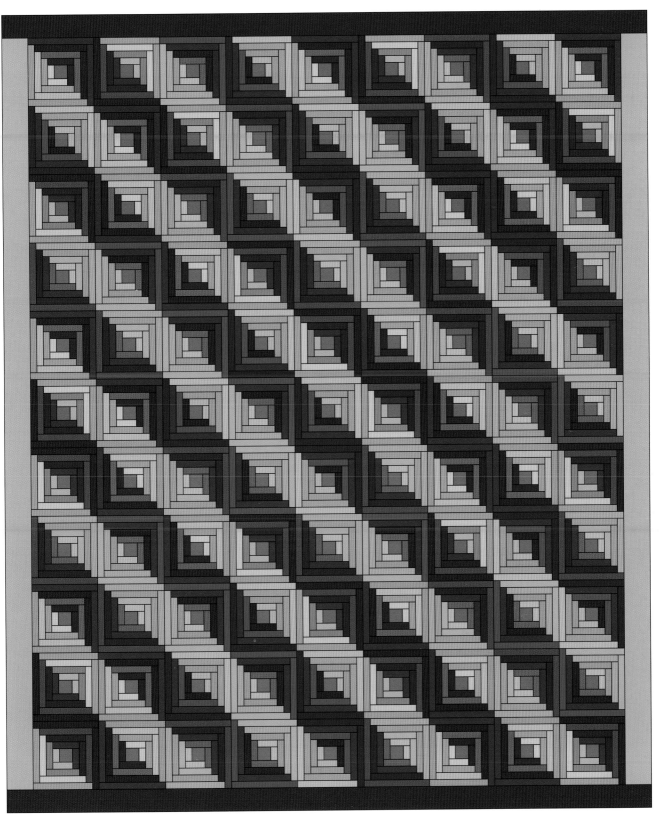

Straight Furrow Quilt

The artistic expertise of nineteenth-century quiltmakers awes us today as we dig into our stash to replicate their naive mastery of design. I often imagine our quilting sisters of long ago tossing light strips into one scrap bag and dark ones into another.

——Marianne

3D Diamonds Quilt

Several Log Cabin variations call for assembling the blocks so that four dark sides come together and four light sides come together, forming a dark/light diamond pattern. The 3D Diamonds pattern uses the traditional single red square representing the "chimney" as the center of the block.

(*Note:* For the quilt projects, some of the dimensions and patterns may have been altered slightly to conform to today's cutting and piecing techniques.)

3D Diamonds

A version of "Sunshine & Shadow," this Michigan quilt is foundation pieced in a variety of woolens and cottons, built around red wool flannel "chimney" blocks. The cottons are roller-printed. The quilt was made around 1880 by Emma Elizabeth Warren of Willis, and donated by an instructor at Scotch Settlement School in the Edison Institute Schools.

Object ID: 71.72.25

3D Diamonds

PROJECT RATING: EASY
Size: 76" x 85½"
Blocks: 72
(9½") Log Cabin blocks

Materials

36 fat quarters★ assorted dark
  prints for blocks
36 fat quarters★ assorted light
  prints for blocks
1 fat quarter★ red solid for block
  centers
⅝ yard dark brown solid for
  binding
5¼ yards backing fabric
Full-size quilt batting
★fat quarter = 18" x 20"

Cutting

Because there are so many pieces
which are similar in size, you may
want to label them as you cut.
Measurements include ¼" seam
allowances.

**From each dark and light fat
  quarter, cut:**

• 12 (1"-wide) strips. From strips,
  cut 2 sets of logs as listed in
  *Cutting Chart for 1 Log Cabin
  Block.*

From red solid, cut:

• 8 (2"-wide) strips. From strips, cut
  72 (2") center squares.

From dark brown solid, cut:

• 9 (2¼"-wide) strips for binding.

Cutting Chart for 1 Log Cabin Block CUT ALL STRIPS 1" WIDE		
DARK STRIPS	**LIGHT STRIPS**	**STRIP LENGTH**
#32		10"
#31	#30	9½"
#28	#29	9"
#27	#26	8½"
#24	#25	8"
#23	#22	7½"
#20	#21	7"
#19	#18	6½"
#16	#17	6
#15	#14	5½"
#12	#13	5"
#11	#10	4½"
#8	#9	4"
#7	#6	3½"
#4	#5	3"
#3	#2	2½"
	#1	2"

Block Assembly

1. Lay out pieces as shown in *Log
Cabin Block Diagram.*

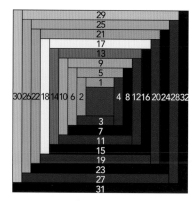

Log Cabin Block Diagram

2. Join strips in numerical order to
complete 1 Log Cabin block. Make
72 Log Cabin blocks.

Quilt Assembly

1. Lay out blocks as shown in *Quilt
Top Assembly Diagram.*
2. Join blocks into horizontal rows;
join rows to complete quilt top.

Finishing

1. Divide backing into 2 (2⅝-yard)
pieces. Divide 1 piece in half
lengthwise to make 2 narrow panels.
Sew 1 narrow panel to each side of
wider panel; press seam allowances
toward narrow panels.
2. Layer backing, batting, and
quilt top; baste. Quilt as desired.
Quilt shown was not quilted.
3. Join 2¼"-wide dark brown strips
into 1 continuous piece for
straight-grain French-fold binding.
Add binding to quilt.

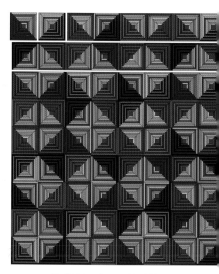

Quilt Top Assembly Diagram

3D Diamonds Quilt

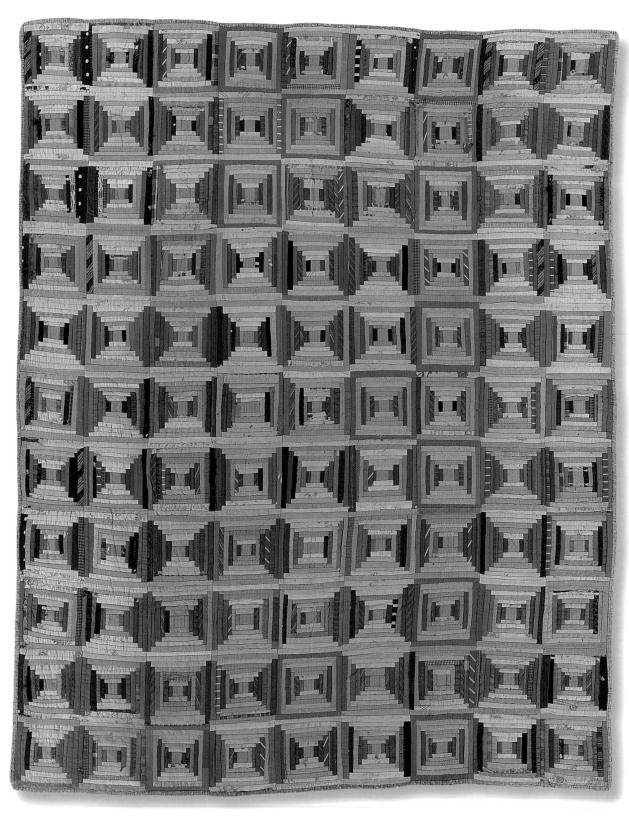

Both of us live in Winterset, the county seat of Madison County, Iowa, with its native limestone courthouse resting solidly in the middle of the town square. We marvel at this stunning quilt design inspired by something so simple as the focus of local government.

—Liz

Courthouse Steps Quilt

In this variation of the Log Cabin design, the dark and light sections of the blocks are placed opposite each other rather than side by side. The central block of the square is not red, which traditionally represents the warmth of the cabin chimney. Instead, the central block is gold, representing the light in the window.

(*Note:* For the quilt projects, some of the dimensions and patterns may have been altered slightly to conform to today's cutting and piecing techniques.)

ourthouse Steps

is utility quilt was hand-pieced
ound 1890, possibly in Canada,
d finished around 1920, with
e addition of machine-sewn cotton
nnel backing and gold yarn ties.
e quilt top is foundation pieced,
ostly with wool but with some
inted cottons, velveteens, and
lks. The quilt has thick batting.

oject ID: 91.0.133.13

Courthouse Steps

PROJECT RATING: EASY
Size: 67½" x 82½"
Blocks: 99 (7½") Log Cabin blocks

Materials

20 fat quarters★ assorted dark prints
   for blocks
25 fat quarters★ assorted light prints
   for blocks
⅜ yard gold solid for block centers
⅝ yard tan print for binding
5 yards backing fabric
Twin-size quilt batting
★fat quarter = 18" x 20"

Cutting

Because there are so many pieces
which are similar in size, you may
want to label them as you cut.
Measurements include ¼" seam
allowances.

From each dark fat quarter, cut:
• 15 (1"-wide) strips. From strips, cut
  5 sets of logs as listed in *Cutting
  Chart for 1 Log Cabin Block.*

From each light fat quarter, cut:
• 16 (1"-wide) strips. From strips, cut
  4 sets of logs as listed in *Cutting
  Chart for 1 Log Cabin Block.*

From gold solid, cut:
• 5 (2"-wide) strips. From strips, cut
  99 (2") center squares.

From tan print, cut:
• 8 (2¼"-wide) strips for binding.

Cutting Chart for 1 Log Cabin Block

CUT ALL STRIPS 1¼" WIDE

DARK STRIPS	LIGHT STRIPS	STRIP LENGTH
	#23, 24	8"
#21, 22	#19, 20	7"
#17, 18	#15, 16	6"
#13, 14	#11, 12	5"
#9, 10	#7, 8	4"
#5, 6	#3, 4	3"
#1, 2		2"

Block Assembly

1. Lay out pieces as shown in *Log
Cabin Block Diagram.*

2. Join strips in numerical order to
complete 1 Log Cabin block. Make
99 Log Cabin blocks.

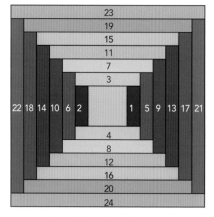

Log Cabin Block Diagram

Quilt Assembly

1. Lay out blocks as shown in *Quilt
Top Assembly Diagram.*

2. Join blocks into horizontal rows;
join rows to complete quilt top.

Finishing

1. Divide backing into 2 (2½-yard)
pieces. Divide 1 piece in half
lengthwise to make 2 narrow panels.
Sew 1 narrow panel to each side of
wider panel; press seam allowances
toward narrow panels.

2. Layer backing, batting, and quilt
top; baste. Quilt as desired. Quilt
shown was tied.

3. Join 2¼"-wide tan print strips
into 1 continuous piece for
straight-grain French-fold binding.
Add binding to quilt.

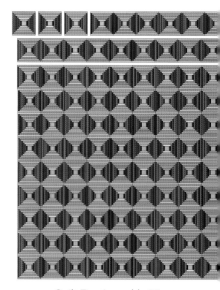

Quilt Top Assembly Diagram

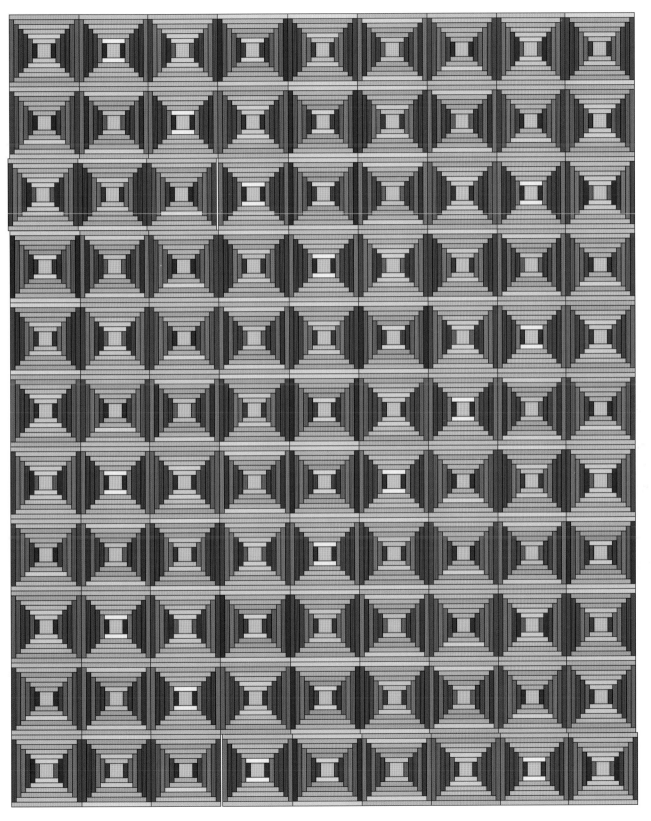

Courthouse Steps Quilt

No Log Cabin selection would be complete without Sunshine & Shadow. The pattern name reflects everyday changes in the weather as well as the nuances of human feeling, the sunshine and shadow, the ups and downs of emotion every person experiences.

——*Marianne*

Sunshine & Shadow Quilt

This version of classic Log Cabin construction,

Sunshine & Shadow, is also known as Light & Dark.

Completed blocks are assembled so that dark meets

dark and light meets light, forming diamonds.

Decorative borders are sometimes added.

(*Note:* For the quilt projects, some of the dimensions and patterns may have been altered slightly to conform to today's cutting and piecing techniques.)

Sunshine & Shadow

This quilt is foundation pieced
n cotton squares, including
oller-printed calicos, with small red
r purple "chimney" squares. The
locks are pieced in wool, silk,
nd cotton, including velvets,
oller-printed patterns, and woven
tripes, plaids, and checks. The quilt
op was sewn by hand around 1880
ut neither quilted nor tied; the
dging was added much later.

Object ID: 00.4.4590

Sunshine & Shadow

PROJECT RATING: EASY
Size: 65⅝" x 84⅜"
Blocks: 63 (9⅜") Log Cabin blocks

Materials
21 fat quarters★ assorted dark
   prints for blocks
21 fat quarters★ assorted light
   prints for blocks
1 fat eighth★★ purple solid for
   block centers
⅝ yard brown solid
   for binding
5¼ yards backing fabric
Twin-size quilt batting
★fat quarter = 18" x 20"
★★fat eighth = 9" x 20"

Cutting
Because there are so many pieces
which are similar in size, you may
want to label them as you cut.
Measurements include ¼" seam
allowances.

**From each dark and light fat
quarter, cut:**
• 15 (1⅛"-wide) strips. From strips,
  cut 3 sets of logs as listed in
  *Cutting Chart for 1 Log Cabin
  Block.*

From purple solid, cut:
• 4 (1⅛"-wide) strips. From strips,
  cut 63 (1⅛") center squares.

From brown solid, cut:
• 8 (2¼"-wide) strips for binding.

Cutting Chart for 1 Log Cabin Block
CUT ALL STRIPS 1¼" WIDE

DARK STRIPS	LIGHT STRIPS	STRIP LENGTH
#28	#27	9⅞"
#24, 26	#23, 25	8⅝"
#20, 22	#19, 21	7⅜"
#16, 18	#15, 17	6⅛"
#12, 14	#11, 13	4⅞"
#8, 10	#7, 9	3⅝"
#4, 6	#3, 5	2⅜"
#2	#1	1⅛"

Block Assembly
1. Lay out pieces as shown in *Log
Cabin Block Diagram.*

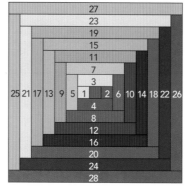

Log Cabin Block Diagram

2. Join strips in numerical order to
complete 1 Log Cabin block. Make
63 Log Cabin blocks.

Quilt Assembly
1. Lay out blocks as shown in *Quilt
Top Assembly Diagram.*
2. Join blocks into horizontal rows;
join rows to complete quilt top.

Finishing
1. Divide backing into 2 (2⅝-yard)
pieces. Divide 1 piece in half
lengthwise to make 2 narrow panels.
Sew 1 narrow panel to each side of
wider panel; press seam allowances
toward narrow panels.
2. Layer backing, batting, and quilt
top; baste. Quilt as desired. Quilt
shown was pieced on a muslin
foundation and was not quilted.
3. Join 2¼"-wide brown strips into
1 continuous piece for straight-grain
French-fold binding. Add binding
to quilt.

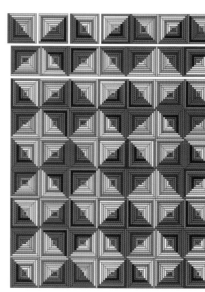

Quilt Top Assembly Diagram

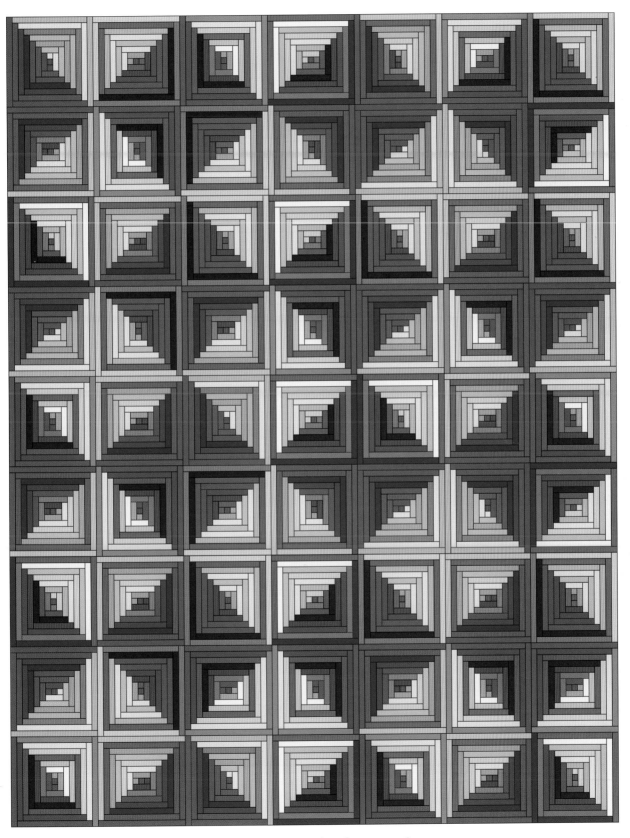

Sunshine & Shadow Quilt

*Zigzag, or Streak of Lightning, may be the liveliest of Log Cabin variations.
Use your darkest scraps for your dark logs and really light scraps, such as
shirting prints, for your light logs, and you will be amazed at the power of
the lightning bolts you create!*

——Liz

Zigzag Quilt

The pattern used in this handsome quilt is also known as Streak of Lightning. Light and dark sides are placed so the top and bottom edges of the quilt are dark, with the "lightning" streaks running through the design. The original quilt is finished with a hand-sewn edging of black silk ribbon.

(*Note:* For the quilt projects, some of the dimensions and patterns may have been altered slightly to conform to today's cutting and piecing techniques.)

Zigzag

The blocks were hand-pieced and then sewn together by machine, around 1890. The solids, plaids, paisleys, and florals are mostly wool, including the traditional red "chimney" blocks. The quilt has dark green wool backing and is tied with dark green and black wool yarn.

Object ID: 00.3.16616

Zigzag

PROJECT RATING: EASY
Size: 61¼" x 70"
Blocks: 56 (8¾") Log Cabin blocks

Materials

19 fat quarters★ assorted dark prints for blocks
14 fat quarters★ assorted light prints for blocks
1 fat quarter★ red solid for block centers
½ yard black solid for binding
3¾ yards backing fabric
Twin-size quilt batting
★fat quarter = 18" x 20"

Cutting

Because there are so many pieces which are similar in size, you may want to label them as you cut. Measurements include ¼" seam allowances.

From each dark fat quarter, cut:
• 12 (1¼"-wide) strips. From strips, cut 3 sets of logs as listed in *Cutting Chart for 1 Log Cabin Block.*

From each light fat quarter, cut:
• 12 (1¼"-wide) strips. From strips, cut 4 sets of logs as listed in *Cutting Chart for 1 Log Cabin Block.*

From red solid, cut:
• 6 (1¾"-wide) strips. From strips, cut 56 (1¾") center squares.

From black solid, cut:
• 7 (2¼"-wide) strips for binding.

Cutting Chart for 1 Log Cabin Block

CUT ALL STRIPS 1¼" WIDE

DARK STRIPS	LIGHT STRIPS	STRIP LENGTH
#20		9¼"
#19	#18	8½"
#16	#17	7¾"
#15	#14	7"
#12	#13	6¼"
#11	#10	5½"
#8	#9	4¾"
#7	#6	4"
#4	#5	3¼"
#3	#2	2½"
	#1	1¾"

Block Assembly

1. Lay out pieces as shown in *Log Cabin Block Diagram.*

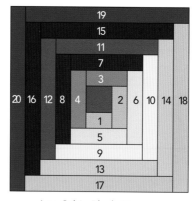

Log Cabin Block Diagram

2. Join strips in numerical order to complete 1 Log Cabin block. Make 56 Log Cabin blocks.

Quilt Assembly

1. Lay out blocks as shown in *Quilt Top Assembly Diagram.*
2. Join blocks into horizontal rows; join rows to complete quilt top.

Finishing

1. Divide backing into 2 (1⅞-yard) pieces. Join panels to make quilt back. Seam will run horizontally.
2. Layer backing, batting, and quilt top; baste. Quilt as desired. Quilt shown was tied.
3. Join 2¼"-wide black solid strips into 1 continuous piece for straight-grain French-fold binding. Add binding to quilt.

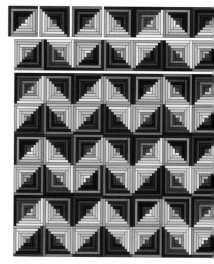

Quilt Top Assembly Diagram

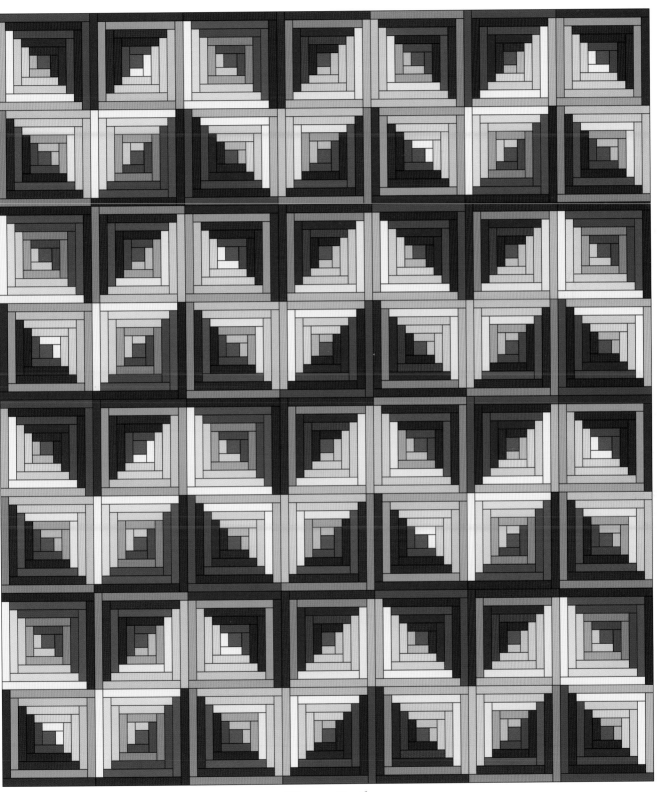

Zizag Quilt

Appliqué
Quilts

offered pioneer women the opportunity to share memories of family and friends through friendship or commemorative designs. Blocks often contained embroidered or even hand-written records of ceremonial events, such as engagements, marriages and births. Many of the quilts offered as quilting projects on the following pages incorporate classic elements of appliqué. The *Star of Bethlehem* quilt is an excellent example of broderie perse—large floral motifs exquisitely cut and appliquéd to the neutral background.

Opposite: A bright appliqué quilt drapes the porch of Sarah Jordan's modest New Jersey boarding house, which accommodated about a dozen of Thomas Edison's bachelor employees. Mrs. Jordan cooked for many more Edison lab workers who fondly recalled her delicious pies.

The sheer exuberance of this remarkable appliqué quilt quickens the pulse and stimulates the soul. If you love needle-turn appliqué, think about recreating this masterpiece, one giant block at a time!

——Marianne

Feather with Flowers Quilt

The unusually dense appliqué and the radiating flowers give a sense of constant movement to this all-cotton quilt top. The pattern shows Pennsylvania German influence, though Pennsylvania quilts were not usually edged with piping. The quilt was made sometime between 1860 and 1890, possibly in Eastern Ohio. Although not made by a member of the Firestone family, it was among items acquired with the Firestone Farmhouse at **The Henry Ford.**

(*Note:* For the quilt projects, some of the dimensions and patterns may have been altered slightly to conform to today's cutting and piecing techniques.)

Feather with Flowers

Four groupings of red and yellow tulips, a central petaled rose, and fern-like foliage are appliquéd, along with additional flower stems radiating from a central rose. Narrow red cotton piping is applied to the hand-sewn edging. The quilting, 11 or 12 stitches to the inch, outlines the appliqué and is in double-line chevrons in the ground area. The quilt was made sometime between 1860 and 1890.

Object ID: 83.1.353

Feather with Flowers

PROJECT RATING: INTERMEDIATE

Size: 88" x 88"

Blocks: 4 (38") blocks

Materials

7 yards white or cream solid for background, border, and binding

4⅜ yards green print for appliqué

2 yards red print for appliqué and piping

¾ yard pink print for appliqué

⅜ yard blue print for appliqué

½ yard yellow print for appliqué

Paper-backed fusible web (optional)

Rug-weight acrylic yarn for piping

Zipper foot or piping foot for sewing machine

Clear monofilament thread

Glue stick

7⅞ yards backing fabric

Queen-size quilt batting

Cutting

Patterns for appliqué are on pages 130–133. Follow manufacturer's instructions if using fusible web. Measurements include ¼" seam allowances. Border strips are exact length needed. You may want to make them longer to allow for piecing variations.

From white solid, cut:

- 4 (38½") background squares.
- 9 (6½"-wide) strips. Piece strips to make 2 (6½" x 88½") top and bottom borders and 2 (6½" x 76½") side borders.
- 10 (2½"-wide) strips for binding.

From green print, cut:

- 1 (38"-long) piece. From piece, cut about 720" of 1⅞"-wide bias strips. Join strips; press in thirds to make folded bias for stems. From folded bias, cut 16 (14"-long) stems and 16 (7½"-long) stems. Remaining folded bias is for vine in border.
- 1 (9"-long) piece. From piece, cut 13 (1⅛"-wide) bias strips. Press strips in thirds to make folded bias for stems. From folded bias strips, cut 52 (3"-long) stems.
- 7 (1¾"-wide) strips for strip sets.
- 16 Feathers.
- 16 Outer Leaves.
- 50 Leaves.
- 39 Leaves reversed.

From red print, cut:

- 7 (1¼"-wide) strips for strip sets.
- 9 (1"-wide) strips for piping.
- 16 Outer Petals.
- 16 Center Petals.
- 4 Medium Flowers.
- 28 Small Flowers.

From pink print, cut:

- 4 Large Flowers.
- 20 Small Flowers.

From blue print, cut:

- 20 Small Flowers.

From yellow print, cut:

- 16 Middle Petals.
- 4 Center Diamonds.
- 68 Centers.

Block Assembly

1. Join 1 (1¾"-wide) green print strip and 1 (1¼"-wide) red print strip to make a strip set (*Strip Set Diagram*).

Make 7 strip sets. From strip sets, cut 47 Pieced Leaves and 66 Pieced Leaves reversed, lining up seam line on pattern with seam of strip set.

Strip Set Diagram

2. Appliqué feathers, leaves, stems, and flowers to block background to complete 1 block (*Block Diagram*). Make 4 blocks.

Block Diagram

Quilt Assembly

1. Referring to *Quilt Top Assembly Diagram*, lay out blocks as shown. Join into horizontal rows; join rows to complete quilt center.

2. Add side borders to quilt center. Add top and bottom borders to quilt.

3. Appliqué leaves, stems, vine, and flowers to border.

inishing

Divide backing into 3 (2⅝-yard)
eces. Join panels lengthwise.
Layer backing, batting, and quilt
p; baste. Quilt as desired. Quilt
own was outline quilted around

appliqué shapes and has a diagonal
grid in the background.

3. Join 2½"-wide white strips into 1
continuous piece for straight-grain
French-fold binding. Join 1"-wide
red print strips into 1 continuous

piece for piping. See *Sew Easy:
Binding with Piping* on page 135 for
instructions to finish quilt with this
detail. Add binding to quilt.

Quilt Top Assembly Diagram

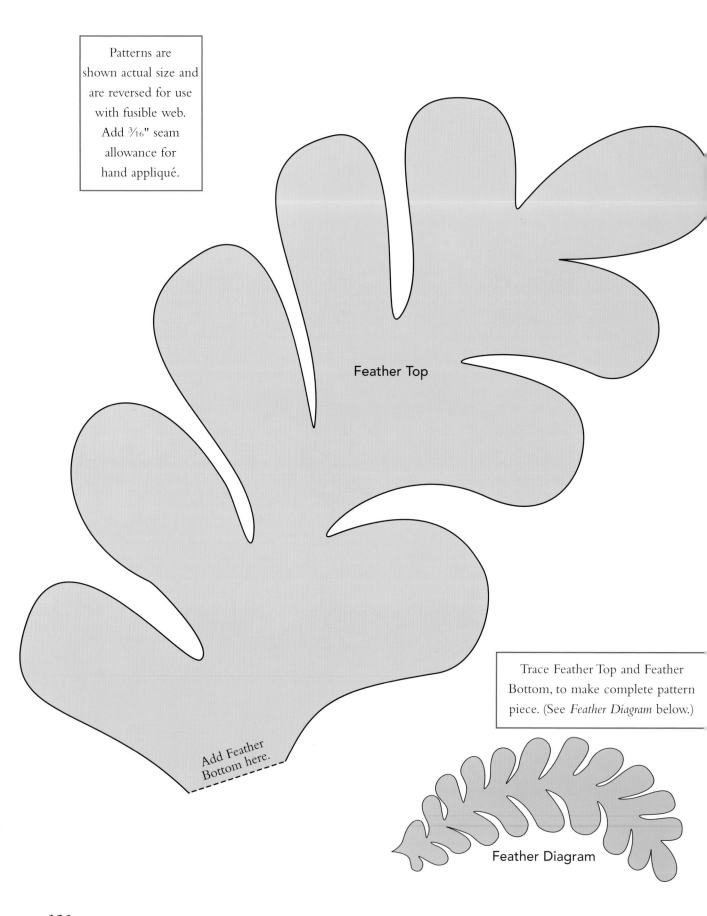

Patterns are shown actual size and are reversed for use with fusible web. Add ³⁄₁₆" seam allowance for hand appliqué.

Feather Top

Add Feather Bottom here.

Trace Feather Top and Feather Bottom, to make complete pattern piece. (See *Feather Diagram* below.)

Feather Diagram

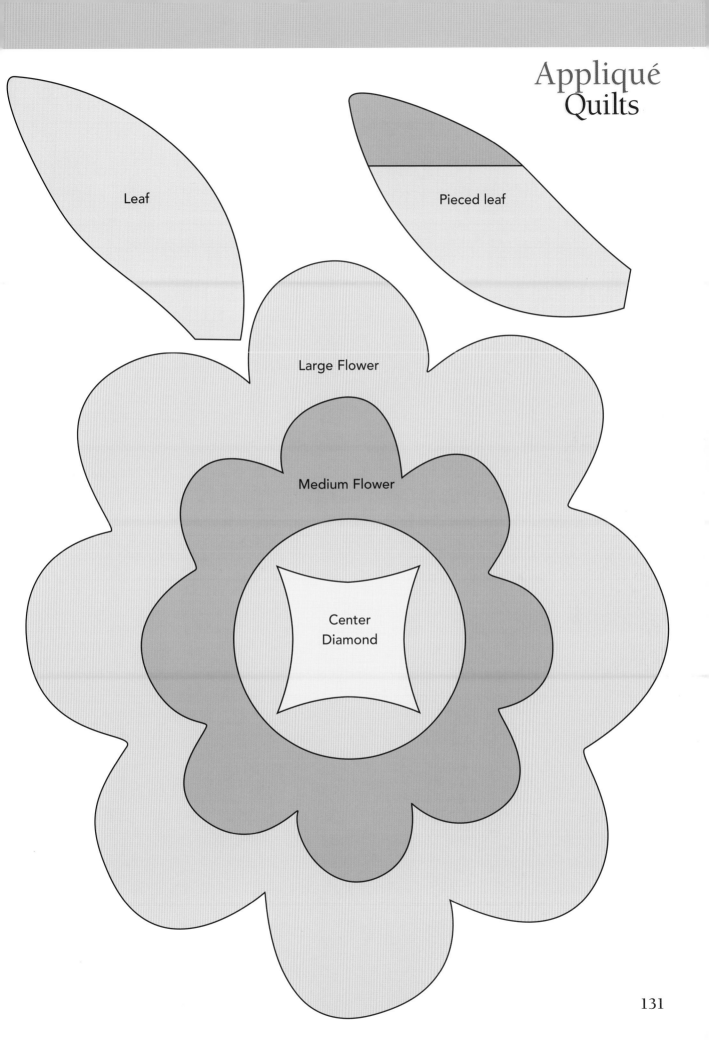

Leaf

Pieced leaf

Large Flower

Medium Flower

Center
Diamond

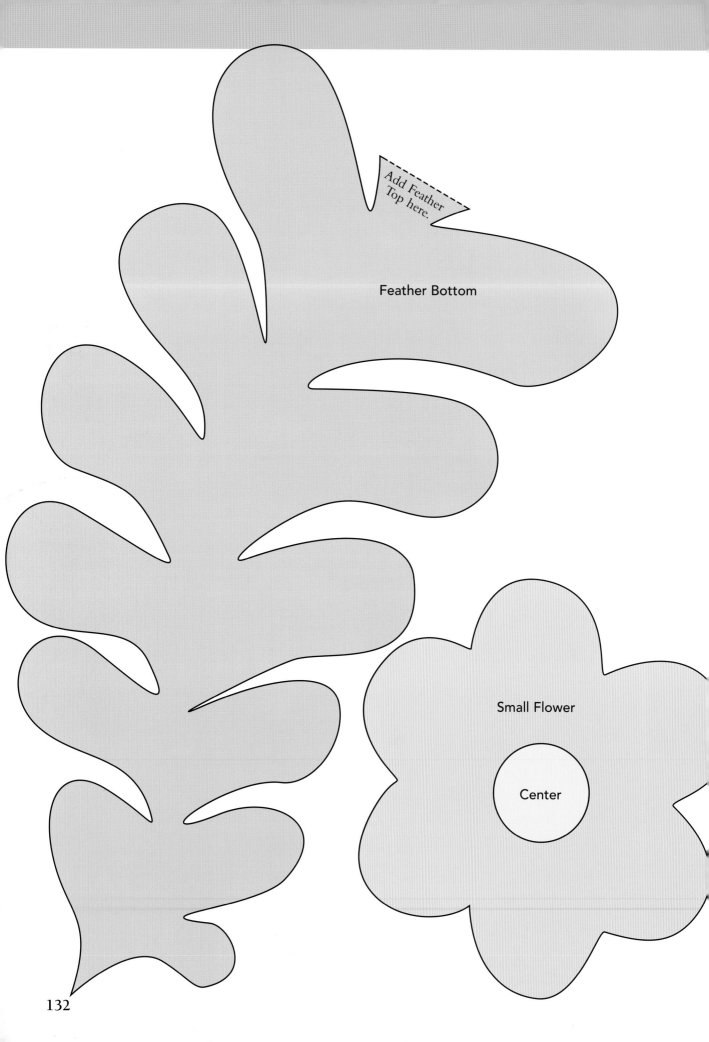

Add Feather Top here.

Feather Bottom

Small Flower

Center

132

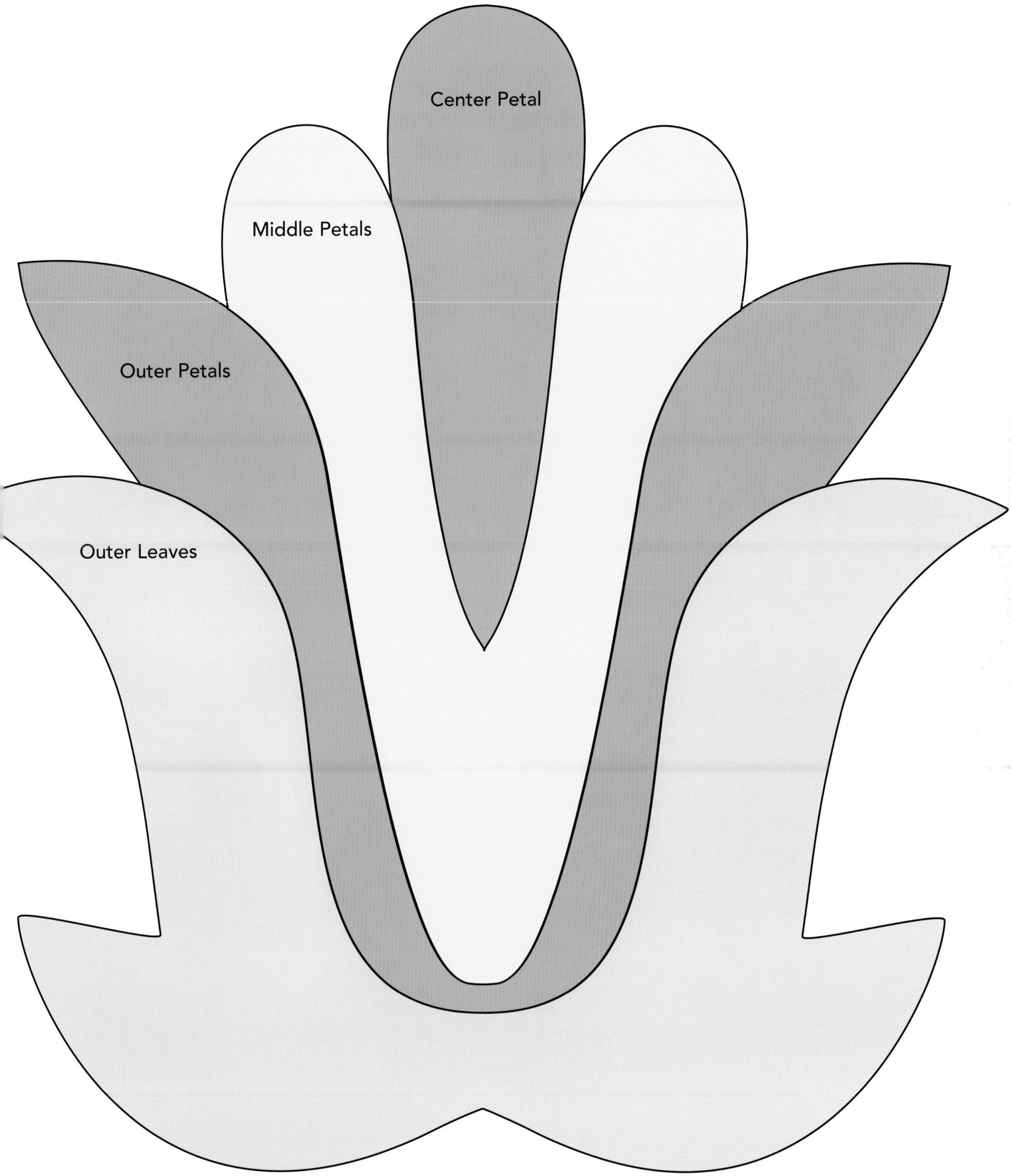

Center Petal

Middle Petals

Outer Petals

Outer Leaves

Feather with Flowers Quilt

Binding with Piping

Narrow piping inserted along the edge of your binding can be the perfect finish for certain projects. Best of all, you can make and finish this binding completely on the sewing machine.

Supplies

Fabric to make 2½"-wide binding

Fabric to make 1"-wide continuous fabric strip to cover yarn piping filler

Rug-weight acrylic yarn

Zipper foot or piping foot for sewing machine

Clear monofilament nylon thread

Glue Stick

Instructions

1. Begin by measuring around the perimeter of your quilt; add 20" to this measurement to allow for mitering corners of binding and finishing the ends. From binding fabric, make 2½"-wide straight-grain binding this length. From piping cover fabric, make 1"-wide straight-grain strip this length.

2. Insert the yarn in the piping cover strip; loosely baste fabric over yarn piping, using zipper or cording foot (Photo A).

3. To mark the center of the binding strip, fold it in half, wrong sides facing, and press. Open binding back out so it is flat; press lightly if desired.

4. Using zipper or cording foot, baste piping to center fold line of binding (Photo B). Fold binding in half with wrong sides facing.

A

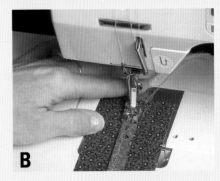

B

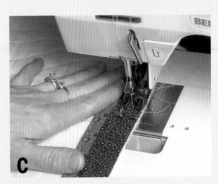

C

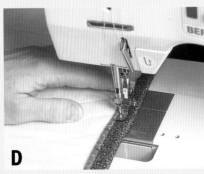

D

Sew Smart™

Use a glue stick to "baste" piping to center fold of binding before stitching. —Marianne

5. Trim excess batting and quilt back so ditch between piping and binding will align with first binding stitching when binding is sewn to quilt.

6. Working from the quilt back, align raw edge of binding with raw edge of quilt back. Piping fabric will be on top of binding fabric. Stitch binding to quilt (Photo C). Miter corners and join the ends just as when applying regular binding.

Sew Smart™

I use my "Liz's Lumpless Binding" technique (May/June 2002 issue of Love of Quilting) to join the ends of the binding. —Liz

7. Bring binding over edge of quilt to front. Use clear monofilament thread (or thread that matches the piping cover fabric) and a zipper or cording foot to topstitch through all layers in the ditch between the piping and the binding (Photo D).

The magnificent "watermelon" appliqué swags that comprise the border for
this quilt are pure American folk art. Use our method for windowing
appliqués if you like to fuse your work—there will be far less bulk in your
finished project.

——Liz

Rose Tree Quilt

Prairie flowers were motifs in quilt patterns variously called Missouri Rose, Rose Tree, or just Prairie Flower. The term "watermelon" as applied to the *Rose Tree* quilt describes the style and color of the swag border, a difficult type of border for which a quilter might use a purchased pattern or template.

(*Note:* For the quilt projects, some of the dimensions and patterns may have been altered slightly to conform to today's cutting and piecing techniques.)

Rose Tree

The arrangement of roses, buds, and foliage is original to the quilter, Ortha Green of Promise City, Iowa, who sewed the quilt around 1935. The border is a "watermelon" swag. The quilt top, batting, and backing all are cotton. The quilting, 9 stitches to the inch, is in diamond crosshatch, feathered circles and swags, stylized pineapples, and outline.

Object ID: 72.42.3

Rose Tree

Size: 75" x 100"

Materials

6 yards cream solid for background
1¾ yards light pink solid for appliqué
1⅝ yard dark pink solid for appliqué and binding
2¾ yards green solid for appliqué
1 fat eighth★ yellow solid for appliqué
Paper-backed fusible web (optional)
6 yards backing fabric
Queen-size quilt batting
★fat eighth = 9" x 20"

Cutting

Patterns for appliqué are on page 138–143. Follow manufacturer's instructions if using fusible web.

From cream solid, cut:
• 2 (3-yard) pieces. Join pieces lengthwise to make background.

From light pink solid, cut:
• 10 (2¼"-wide) strips for binding.
• 10 Swags.
• 4 Corner Oval 3.
• 6 Large Flowers.
• 22 C.
• 22 C reversed.

From dark pink solid, cut:
• 10 Swags.
• 4 Corner Oval 2.
• 6 Small Flower.
• 22 B.
• 22 B reversed.

From green solid, cut:
• 1 (24"-long) piece. From piece, cut about 250" of 2¼"-wide bias strips. Join strips; press in thirds to make folded bias for stems. From folded bias, cut 6 (32"-long) stems, 12 (3"-long) stems, and 4 (2"-long) stems.
• 10 Swags.
• 4 Corner Oval 1.
• 22 A.
• 22 D.
• 22 D reversed.
• 22 E.
• 22 E reversed.
• 28 F.
• 6 bases.
• 114 leaves.

From yellow solid, cut:
• 6 centers.
• 4 Corner Oval 4.

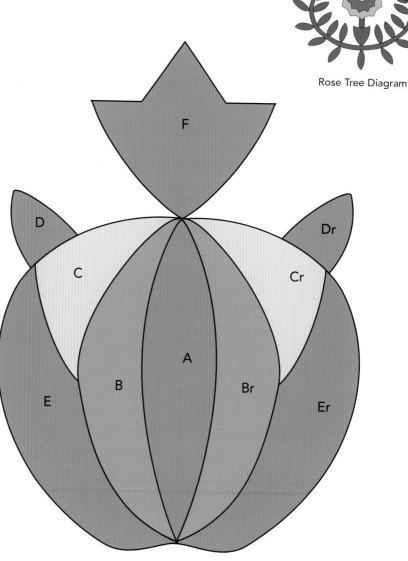

Rose Tree Diagram

Rose

138

Quilt Assembly

1. Referring to *Quilt Top Assembly Diagram*, lay out pieces on background as shown. Appliqué pieces to background.

2. Trim background to 75" x 100".

Finishing

1. Divide backing into 2 (3-yard) pieces. Divide 1 piece in half lengthwise to make 2 narrow panels. Join 1 narrow panel to each side of wider panel; press seam allowances toward narrow panels.

2. Layer backing, batting, and quilt top; baste. Quilt as desired. Quilt shown was outline quilted around the appliqué shapes and on the swags and has feather designs and a diagonal grid in the background.

3. Join 2¼"-wide light pink strips into 1 continuous piece for straight-grain French-fold binding. Add binding to quilt.

Quilt Top Assembly Diagram

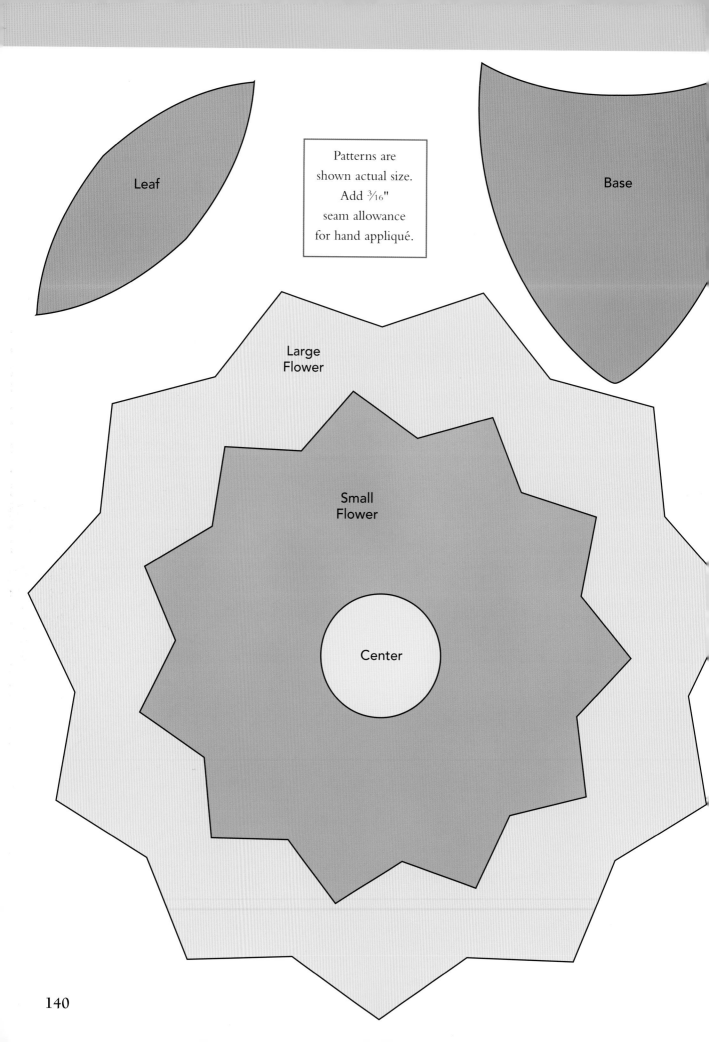

Leaf

Base

Patterns are
shown actual size.
Add ³⁄₁₆"
seam allowance
for hand appliqué.

Large
Flower

Small
Flower

Center

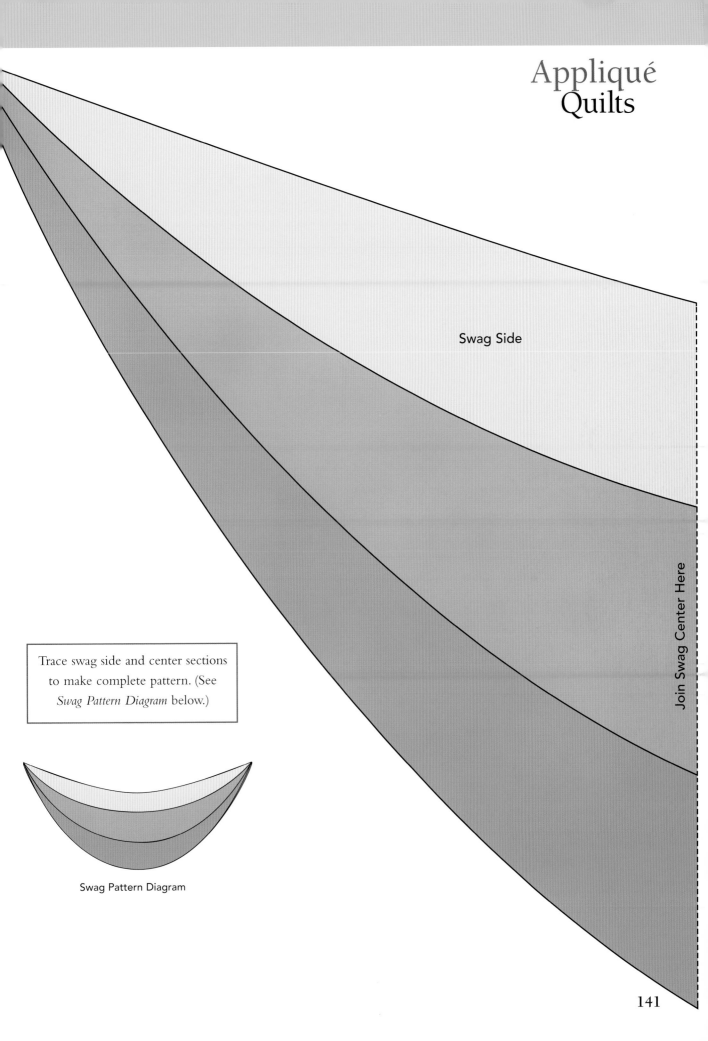

Swag Side

Join Swag Center Here

Trace swag side and center sections
to make complete pattern. (See
Swag Pattern Diagram below.)

Swag Pattern Diagram

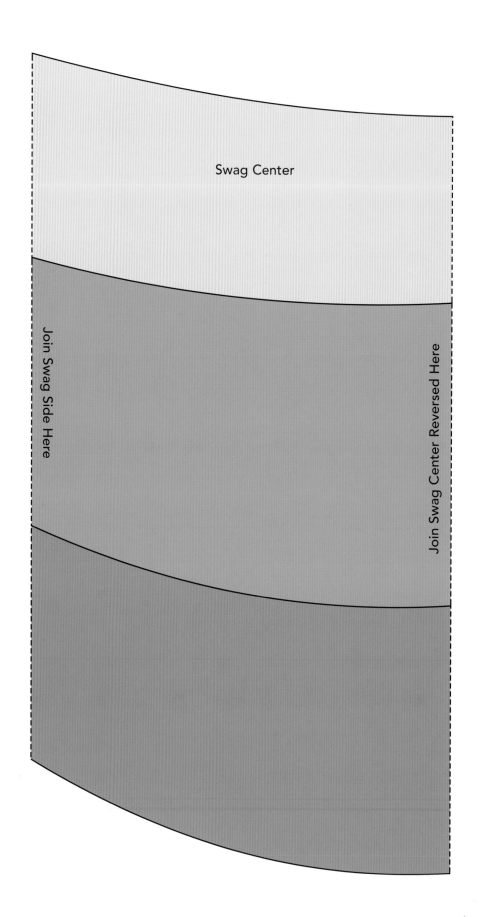

Swag Center

Join Swag Side Here

Join Swag Center Reversed Here

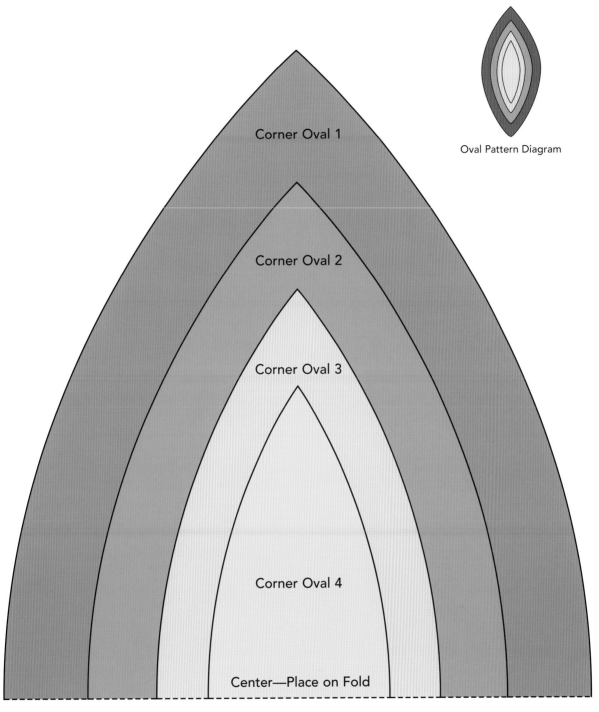

Oval Pattern Diagram

Corner Oval 1

Corner Oval 2

Corner Oval 3

Corner Oval 4

Center—Place on Fold

Corner Ovals

Rose Tree Quilt

Windowing Fusible Appliqués

ry our method for utilizing fusible web that keeps appliqués soft nd flexible. It's perfect for the *Rose Tree* quilt on page 136.

hoose a lightweight "sewable" sible web product. Ask the staff your favorite quilt shop to commend brands. Always read and llow manufacturer's instructions for sing time and iron temperature.

 w Smart™

used shapes will be the reverse of e pattern you trace. If it's impor-nt for an object to face a certain irection, make a reverse pattern to ace. We do this quickly by tracing e design on tracing paper, then rning the paper over and tracing e design through onto the other de of the paper. —Marianne

. Use a pencil to trace appliqué otifs onto the paper side of the sible web, making a separate acing for each appliqué you need *Photo A)*.

. Roughly cut out drawn appliqué apes, cutting to the outside of awn lines *(Photo B)*.

3. "Window" the fusible by trimming out the interior of the shape, leaving a scant ¼" to the inside of the drawn line *(Photo C)*. Follow manufacturer's instructions to fuse the web side of each shape to the wrong side of the appliqué fabric.

4. Cut out appliqués, cutting carefully on drawn outline *(Photo D)*. Only a thin band of fusible web frames each shape.

5. Peel off paper backing *(Photo E)*. Position appliqués in place on background fabric, and follow manufacturer's instructions to fuse shapes in place.

Sew Smart™

If you have trouble peeling the paper backing, try scoring paper with a pin to give you an edge to begin with. —Liz

A

B

C

D

E

*Friendship is as important to quilters now as it was in the nineteenth century.
Long ago, quilters inked their names onto pieces of fabric because they wished
to stay connected to each other. Quilters today still exchange signatures and
trade blocks for friendship quilts.*

——Marianne

Reel Variation Quilt

The friendship quilt was a popular gift throughout the middle of the 1800s. Each block of this *Reel Variation* quilt bears a name and some decorative device, printed or written in ink. Such a friendship quilt might be presented to a bride or to a young man when he turned eighteen. During the era of national expansion, a friendship quilt might travel with someone who was leaving for the west.

(*Note:* For the quilt projects, some of the dimensions and patterns may have been altered slightly to conform to today's cutting and piecing techniques.)

Reel Variation

This appliquéd and pieced quilt was made in Bucks County, Pennsylvania around 1846, possibly by Quakers. It features a wonderful assortment of early roller-printed, wood-block printed, discharge, and over-printed cottons. A square grid sashing sets off the 49 pattern blocks. The red block centers are made from many different prints. The quilting is 7 to 9 stitches to the inch, done in white thread.

Object ID: 79.32.1

Reel Variation

PROJECT RATING: EASY
Size: 103½" x 103½"
Blocks: 49 (11") Reel blocks

Materials

25 fat quarters★★ assorted red prints for blocks
25 fat eighths★ assorted green, blue, and brown prints for blocks
5¾ yards cream solid for background
3¾ yards brown print for sashing (extra yardage may be required if using a vertical stripe fabric)
1¾ yards blue print for border and binding
Paper-backed fusible web (optional)
9 yards backing fabric
King-size quilt batting
★fat eighth = 9" x 20"
★★fat quarter = 18" x 20"

Cutting

Patterns for appliqué are on page 149. Follow manufacturer's instructions if using fusible web. Measurements include ¼" seam allowances. Border strips are exact length needed. You may want to make them longer to allow for piecing variations.

From each fat quarter, cut:
• 2 center pieces.
From each fat eighth, cut:
• 16 petals.
From cream solid, cut:
• 17 (11½"-wide) strips. From strips, cut 49 (11½") background squares.
From brown print, cut:
• 12 (3¼"-wide) **lengthwise** strips. From strips, cut 2 (3¼" x 99½") long horizontal sashing strips, 8 (3¼" x 94") vertical sashing strips, and 42 (3¼" x 11½") short horizontal sashing strips.
From blue print, cut:
• 12 (2¾"-wide) strips. Piece strips to make 2 (2¾" x 104") top and bottom borders and 2 (2¾" x 99½") side borders.
• 11 (2¼"-wide) strips for binding.

Block Assembly

1. Choose 1 red center piece and 8 matching petals. Appliqué pieces to block background to complete 1 Reel block (*Block Diagram*).
2. Make 49 blocks.

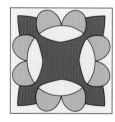

Block Diagram

Quilt Assembly

1. Referring to *Quilt Top Assembly Diagram*, lay out blocks and sashing strips as shown. Join into vertical rows; join rows to complete quilt center.

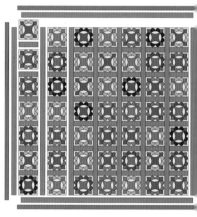

Quilt Top Assembly Diagram

2. Add blue side borders to quilt center. Add blue top and bottom borders to quilt.

Finishing

1. Divide backing into 3 (3-yard) pieces. Join panels lengthwise to make backing.
2. Layer backing, batting, and quilt top; baste. Quilt as desired. Quilt shown was outline quilted around the appliqué and has diagonal lines in the sashing and border.
3. Join 2¼"-wide blue print strips into 1 continuous piece for straight-grain French–fold binding. Add binding to quilt.

Appliqué
Quilts

Patterns are
shown actual size.
Add ³⁄₁₆"
seam allowance
for hand appliqué.

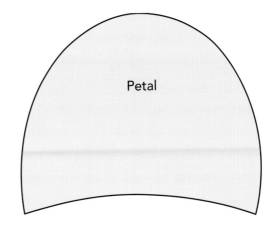

Petal

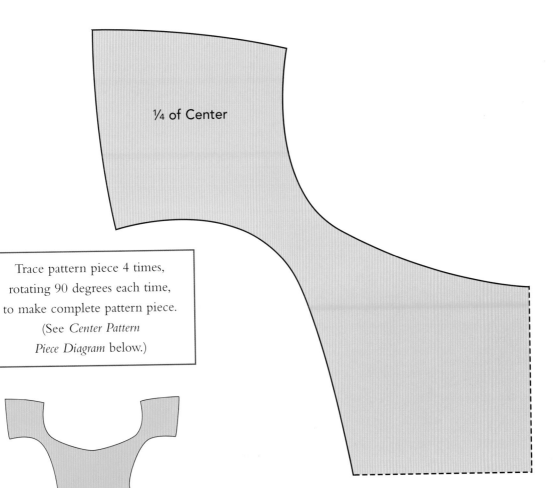

¼ of Center

Trace pattern piece 4 times,
rotating 90 degrees each time,
to make complete pattern piece.
(See *Center Pattern
Piece Diagram* below.)

Center Pattern Piece Diagram

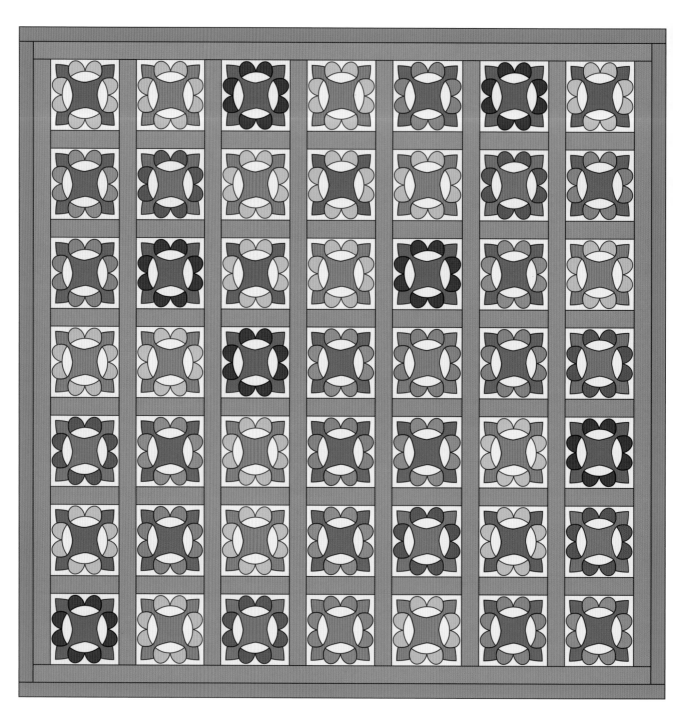

Reel Variation Quilt

Sew Easy™

Tips for Satin Stitch Machine Appliqué

Try these tricks to give your satin stitch machine appliqué projects a professional appearance.

Stabilizers

Stabilizing may be necessary on an appliqué project to prevent puckering. In *Photo A* the stitching on the left has no stabilizer, and there is visible "tunneling" of the fabric. The stitching on the right has stabilizer and is smooth. Stabilizers (*Photo B*) are available in several varieties including tear-away, cut-away, and water-soluble. For some projects, 2 layers of a lightweight stabilizer will be easier to remove than 1 layer of a heavyweight stabilizer.

Zigzag Stitching Curves

Stop with your needle down on the outside of an outer curve, pivot slightly, and continue stitching, stopping to pivot as necessary. Stop with needle down on the inside of an inner curve, pivot, and continue stitching and pivoting (*Diagram C*). *Photo D* shows incorrect pivoting that results in gaps in the satin stitching.

Zigzag Stitching Points

Gradually reduce the width of your zigzag stitch to near zero as you approach the point (*Diagram E*). Pivot at the point and resume stitching, increasing the stitch width until you meet the previous line of stitching. Then, continue stitching. *Photo F* shows incorrect stitching with stitch buildup at the point.

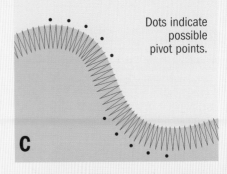
Dots indicate possible pivot points.

C

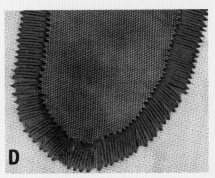

D

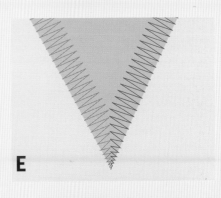

E

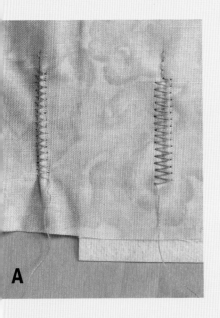

A

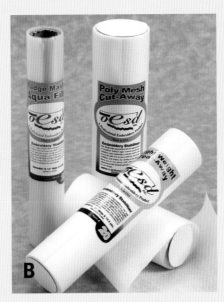

B

F

This classic of American nineteenth-century quiltmaking style utilizes a small number of fabrics. The appliqué shapes are easy motifs. You'll need only a reproduction yellow-green, a Turkey red, and unbleached muslin. ——Liz

Laurel Leaf Cross Quilt

The arrangement of this four-branch floral and foliage design is a common floral appliqué treatment. Branches arranged in an X shape end in red buds; four buds meet to form the flower. The style of this quilt's borders—a series of delicate narrow strips and one wide strip—points to an origin in Ohio.

(*Note:* For the quilt projects, some of the dimensions and patterns may have been altered slightly to conform to today's cutting and piecing techniques.)

Laurel Leaf Cross

The quilt may have been made around 1860, although the square style is from an earlier date. It is all cotton and hand sewn. The appliqué is a green with brown print calico and a red and white print calico, on a white ground. The quilting is extremely close, a diamond crosshatch in open areas and diagonal lines (only ¼" apart) in the appliqué.

Object ID: 74.128.2

Laurel Leaf Cross

PROJECT RATING: EASY
Size: 76½" x 76½"
Blocks: 9 (20") Laurel Leaf blocks

Materials

4¾ yards white or cream solid for background, border, and binding
3½ yards green print for appliqué and borders
¾ yard red print for appliqué and border
Paper-backed fusible web (optional)
4¾ yards backing fabric
Full-size quilt batting

Cutting

Patterns for appliqué are on page 155. Follow manufacturer's instructions if using fusible web. Measurements include ¼" seam allowances. Border strips are exact length needed. You may want to make them longer to allow for piecing variations.

From white solid, cut:
• 5 (20½"-wide) strips. From strips, cut 9 (20½") background squares.
• 8 (4½"-wide) strips. Piece strips to make 2 (4½" x 75½") top and bottom Border 4 and 2 (4½" x 67½") side Border 4.
• 8 (2¼"-wide) strips for binding.

From green print, cut:
• 1 (24"-long) piece. From piece, cut about 405" of 1⅛"-wide bias strips. Join strips; press in thirds to make folded bias for stems. From folded bias, cut 18 (22½"-long) stems.

• 16 (1¾"-wide) strips. Piece strips to make 2 (1¾" x 67½") top and bottom Border 3, 2 (1¾" x 65") side Border 3, 2 (1¾" x 63") top and bottom Border 1, and 2 (1¾" x 60½") side Border 1.
• 8 (1¼"-wide) strips. Piece strips to make 2 (1¼" x 77") top and bottom Border 5 and 2 (1¼" x 75½") side Border 5.
• 144 leaves.

From red print, cut:
• 8 (1½"-wide) strips. Piece strips to make 2 (1½" x 65") top and bottom Border 2 and 2 (1½" x 63") side Border 2.
• 72 petals.

Block Assembly

1. Appliqué stems, leaves, and petals to block background to complete 1 Laurel Leaf block *(Block Diagram)*.
2. Make 9 blocks.

Block Diagram

Quilt Assembly

1. Referring to *Quilt Top Assembly Diagram*, lay out blocks as shown. Join into horizontal rows; join rows to complete quilt center.
2. Add green Border 1 to sides of quilt center. Add green Border 1 to top and bottom of quilt.
3. Repeat for Borders 2, 3, 4, and 5.

Finishing

1. Divide backing into 2 (2⅜-yard) pieces. Divide 1 piece in half lengthwise to make 2 narrow panels. Sew 1 narrow panel to each side of wider panel; press seam allowances toward narrow panels.
2. Layer backing, batting, and quilt top; baste. Quilt as desired. Quilt shown was quilted with an allover diagonal grid.
3. Join 2¼"-wide white strips into 1 continuous piece for straight-grain French-fold binding. Add binding to quilt.

Quilt Top Assembly Diagram

Appliqué patterns are shown finished size. Add ³⁄₁₆" seam allowance for hand appliqué.

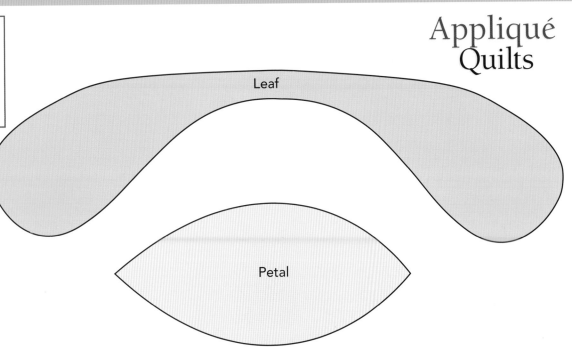

Leaf

Petal

Laurel Leaf Cross Quilt

*We love the originality of this Oak Leaf and Reel variation. It was made
in the middle of the nineteenth century, when any quilter worth her salt was
appliquéing in red and green!*

——*Marianne*

Old Leaf Wreath Quilt

The pattern of this large quilt may be an Oak Leaf variation. Four arms, each with four petals, radiate from the centers of the sixteen blocks, each quilted in white thread with a feathered wreath, a square crosshatch center, and foliage forms in the corners. The border is quilted in an overall clamshell pattern. To finish her work, the quilter brought the edges back to the top.

(*Note:* For the quilt projects, some of the dimensions and patterns may have been altered slightly to conform to today's cutting and piecing techniques.)

Old Leaf Wreath

The top is hand-sewn in three roller-printed patterns: red with dots and stars, gold and blue floral, and green floral. The meandering vine border, with its varied leaves and flowers, is made of the same fabrics. The quilt, which has "H.J." cross-stitched in two corners, was made between 1825 and 1875; chrome orange and stylized motifs point to 1850 as a probable date.

Object ID: 57.17.11

Old Leaf Wreath

PROJECT RATING: INTERMEDIATE
Size: 84" x 84"
Blocks: 16 (16") Wreath blocks

Materials

7 yards cream solid for background
  and binding
1⅞ yards red print for appliqué
¾ yard gold print for appliqué
2⅜ yards green print for appliqué
Paper-backed fusible web (optional)
7½ yards backing fabric
Queen-size quilt batting

Cutting

Patterns for appliqué are on page
159–160. Follow manufacturer's
instructions if using fusible web.
Measurements include ¼" seam
allowances.

From cream solid, cut:

• 8 (16½"-wide) strips. From strips,
  cut 16 (16½") background squares.
•8 (10½"-wide) strips. Piece strips to
  make 2 (10½" x 64½") side borders and 2 (10½" x 84½") top and
  bottom borders.
• 9 (2¼"-wide) strips for binding.

From red print, cut:

• 64 Flower 2.
• 14 Flower 4.
• 14 Flower 4 reversed.

From gold print, cut:

• 16 Flower 1.
• 28 Flower 3.

From green print, cut:

• 1 (18"-long) piece. From piece, cut
  340" of ¾"-wide bias strips. Press
  strips in thirds for vine.
• 64 Leaf 1.
• 14 Leaf 2.
• 14 Leaf 2 reversed.
• 112 Leaf 3.

Block Assembly

1. Choose 1 gold print Flower 1, 4
red print Flower 2, and 4 green print
Leaf 1. Appliqué pieces on block
background to complete 1 Wreath
block *(Block Diagram)*.
2. Make 16 blocks.

Block Diagram

Quilt Assembly

1. Referring to *Quilt Top Assembly
Diagram*, lay out blocks as shown.
Join into horizontal rows; join rows
to complete quilt center.

2. Add cream side borders to quilt
center. Add cream top and bottom
borders to quilt.
3. Referring to *Quilt Top Assembly
Diagram*, appliqué vine, flowers and
leaves on border.

Finishing

1. Divide backing into 3 (2½-yard)
pieces. Join panels lengthwise.
2. Layer backing, batting, and quilt
top; baste. Quilt as desired. Quilt
shown was quilted with feather
designs in the blocks, and clamshells
in the border.
3. Join 2¼"-wide cream strips into
continuous piece for straight-grain
French-fold binding. Add binding
to quilt.

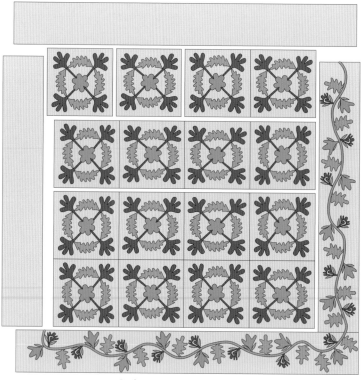

Quilt Top Assembly Diagram

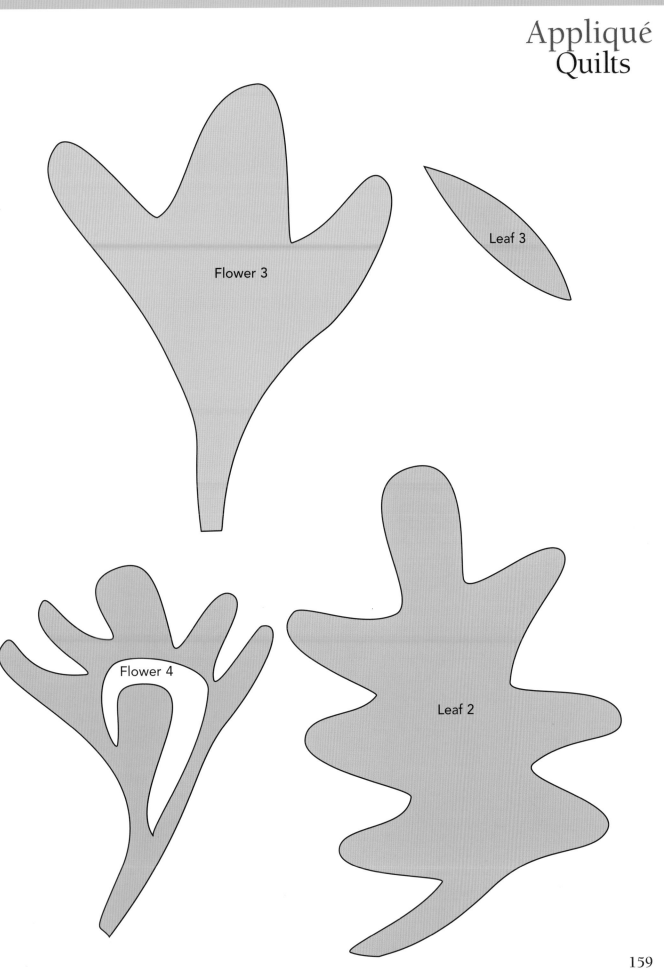

Flower 3

Leaf 3

Flower 4

Leaf 2

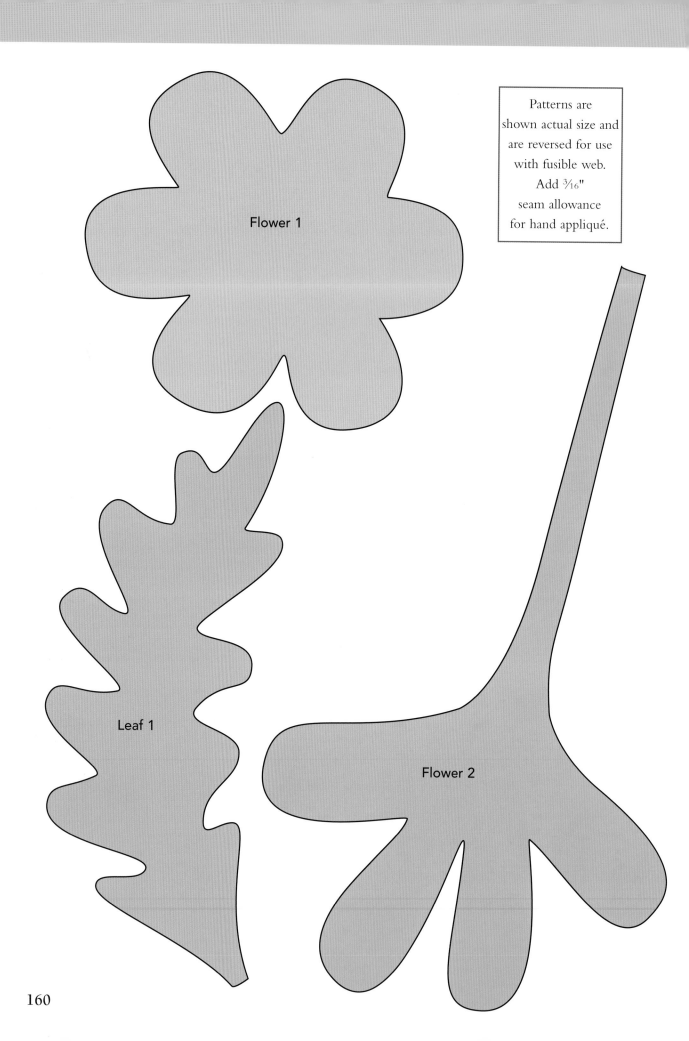

Flower 1

Patterns are
shown actual size and
are reversed for use
with fusible web.
Add ³⁄₁₆"
seam allowance
for hand appliqué.

Leaf 1

Flower 2

160

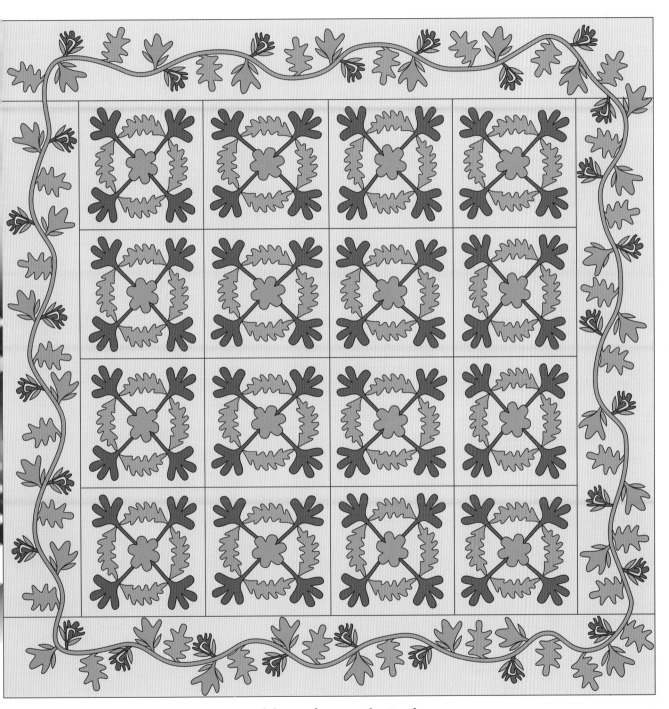

Old Leaf Wreath Quilt

Patchwork Quilts

gained popularity with women who had little time for appliqué but wanted to express their creativity. Quilt blocks could be made one at a time and carried almost everywhere—even in the confines of a covered wagon. Later quilters began sharing blocks through quilting "parties." Names for the block patterns emerged from surroundings and from quilters' block exchanges. Several block patterns such as Peony, Pineapple, Lady of the Lake, and Postage Stamp are featured in the quilting projects offered in this chapter. They have been favorites of quilters through the generations.

Opposite: The *Sunburst* quilt reflects the power and energy of the Loranger Gristmill, from Monroe, Michigan. The circa 1832 mill was remarkably mechanized—conveyor belts moved the grain up, down, and around the building.

Discover (or rediscover) the joys of hand piecing, and connect with the past as you cut and sew the units for this spectacular quilt. Bring the design into the present by choosing a different batik fabric from your stash for each of the Sunburst blocks.

—Liz

Sunburst Quilt

By its size and petal arrangement, the Sunburst pattern is well suited for use as a quilt motif that can be neatly arranged in rows, as in this diagonal design. Some of the prints in this vintage quilt use bright blue with browns or tans, a color combination that was popular from around 1830 to 1860.

(*Note:* For the quilt projects, some of the dimensions and patterns may have been altered slightly to conform to today's cutting and piecing techniques.)

Sunburst

ts colors and border suggest that his quilt was made in New England, ossibly around 1840. It is pieced in variety of wood-block printed lorals, stripes, plaids, and other atterns. The border is pieced riangles in white, red-and-white mall checks, and a green seaweed rint that is also used in several locks. The quilting is in white hread, 7 to 9 stitches to the inch.

Object ID: 73.205.17

Patchwork Sunburst

PROJECT RATING: CHALLENGING
Size: 97½" x 97½"
Blocks: 61 (10") Sunburst blocks

Materials

11¾ yards cream solid for blocks, background, and border
19 fat quarters★ assorted blue, red, green, brown, and gold prints for blocks
¾ yard red print for blocks and border
¾ yard green print for blocks and border
⅞ yard red-and-white print for binding
2 yards lightweight washable interfacing for lining block centers
Template material
9 yards backing fabric
King-size quilt batting
★fat quarter = 18" x 20"

Cutting

Patterns for templates are on page 168. Measurements include ¼" seam allowances.

From cream solid, cut:
- 3 (16¾"-wide) strips. From strips, cut 6 (16¾") squares. Cut squares in half diagonally in both directions to make 24 quarter-square side setting triangles.
- 20 (11½"-wide) strips. From strips, cut 60 (11½") background squares.
- 214 E triangles for border.
- 1098 B triangles for blocks.
- 1098 C triangles for blocks.

From each fat quarter, cut:
- 3 (5") squares for block centers.
- 54 A diamonds for blocks.

From red print, cut:
- 2 (5") squares for block centers.
- 36 A diamonds for blocks.
- 106 E triangles for border.

From green print, cut:
- 2 (5") squares for block centers.
- 36 A diamonds for blocks.
- 108 E triangles for border.

From red-and-white print, cut:
- 11 (2¼"-wide) strips for binding.

From interfacing, cut:
- 61 (5") squares.

Block Assembly

1. Choose 1 set of 18 matching A diamonds and 1 (5") square. Lay out 1 A diamond, 1 cream B triangle, and 1 cream C triangle, right sides facing up, as shown in *Layout Diagram*. Put pieces right sides together just before you sew.

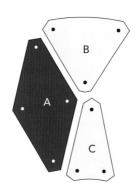

Layout Diagram

2. Join C to A, stitching from edge to edge *(Assembly Diagram 1)*. Press seam allowance away from diamond.

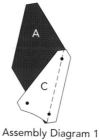

Assembly Diagram 1

3. Paying careful attention to add B to correct side of diamond, place pieces so that diamond is atop B and wrong side up. In this position, the previous stitching line on the diamond can be used as the starting guide to add B. Join A to B, stitching from previous stitching line to outer edge *(Assembly Diagram 2)*. Press seam allowance away from diamond. Make 18 A/B/C units *(A/B/C Unit Diagram)*.

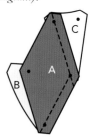

Assembly Diagram 2

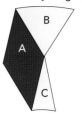

A/B/C Unit Diagram

4. Referring to *Assembly Diagram 3*, join B piece of 1 A/B/C Unit to A diamond of another unit. Begin stitching at dot where the 3 pieces of the first unit meet and sew to the edge of the unit. Press seam allowance away from diamond.

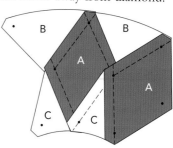

Assembly Diagram 3

. Finish joining the 2 units by
itching the C piece to the
me diamond. Sew from edge to
enter dot. Press seam allowances
oward diamond.

. Continue to join A/B/C Units in
his manner until all units are joined
nto a ring *(Assembly Diagram 4)*.
ress seam allowances consistently.

Assembly Diagram 4

. Stay-stitch ¼" from outside edge
f ring. Press under seam allowance
long stitching. Do not turn under
dge on inside circle.

. Trace D circle on wrong side of 1
quare of interfacing. Cut a 1"–2" slit
n the center of drawn circle. Place
nterfacing and (5") square of print
abric right sides together. Using a
mall sewing machine stitch, stitch
round entire circle on drawn line.
rim and clip seam allowance. Turn
he circle right side out through slit.
enter and appliqué on ring to
omplete Sunburst block *(Sunburst
Diagram)*. Make 61 Sunburst blocks.

Sunburst Diagram

Quilt Assembly

1. Lay out cream background
squares and setting triangles as
shown in *Quilt Top Assembly Diagram*.
Join into diagonal rows; join rows to
complete background.

2. Center and baste 1 Sunburst
block at each intersection where
4 blocks or setting triangles
come together. Appliqué block to
background. Trim away background
fabric from behind Sunburst blocks.

3. Join 53 cream E triangles, 26 red
print E triangles, and 26 green print
E triangles as shown in *Border
Assembly Diagram* to complete 1 side
border. Make 2 side borders.
Measure length of quilt and trim
side borders to this measurement.
Add borders to sides of quilt.

4. Join 54 cream E triangles, 27 red
print E triangles, and 28 green
print E triangles to complete top

border. Repeat for bottom border.
Measure width of quilt, including
side borders, and trim top and
bottom borders to this measurement.
Add borders to quilt.

Border Assembly Diagram

Finishing

1. Divide backing into 3 (3-yard)
pieces. Join panels lengthwise.

2. Layer backing, batting, and quilt
top; baste. Quilt as desired. Quilt
shown has flowers in centers of
blocks and background squares, a
diagonal grid in background, and
straight lines in border.

3. Join 2¼" red-and-white print
strips into 1 continuous piece for
straight-grain French-fold binding.
Add binding to quilt.

Quilt Top Assembly Diagram

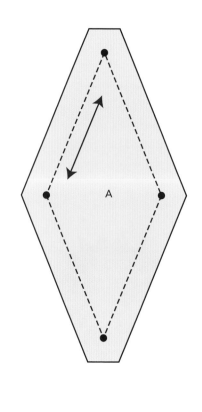

A

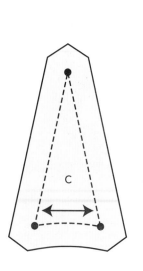

C

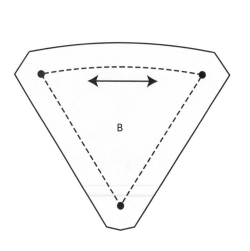

B

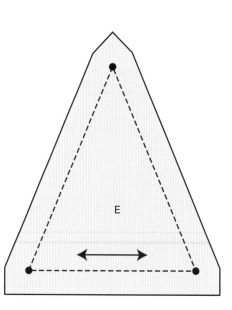

E

D

Sunburst Quilt

This large quilt was undoubtedly created with great pride. One wonders what quiltmaker Henrietta Wilson might have made today were she handed a rotary cutter, mat, and an unlimited supply of cotton prints! Our instructions call for strip sets that greatly speed up the construction of the large star.——Marianne

Star of Bethlehem Quilt

This impressive *Star of Bethlehem* quilt features excellent examples of broderie perse and exquisitely pieced star points throughout. The quilt was made around 1850 by Henrietta Johnson Wilson, wife of Dr. Daniel Wilson of Louisville, Kentucky, and was obtained from the maker's granddaughter, Anne Wilson Anderson.

(*Note:* For the quilt projects, some of the dimensions and patterns may have been altered slightly to conform to today's cutting and piecing techniques.)

Star of Bethlehem

The star is made of diamond-shaped cottons in wood-block, copper-plate, and roller prints of florals and dots, on a white ground. The spaces formed by the star have glazed chintz appliqués of a pheasant and foliage.

Object ID: 72.41.1

Star of Bethlehem

Size: 111⅝" x 111⅝"

Materials

5¼ yards cream solid for background, center medallion, and pieced border

2½ yards tan print for center and pieced border

1½ yards brown print for center and binding

¾ yard pink print for center

2 yards red print for center and pieced border

⅝ yard light teal print for center

¾ yard dark teal print for center

2½ yards large-scale print for broderie perse appliqué (or enough for 8 motifs)

3 yards multi-color print for borders

Paper-backed fusible web

Template material

10 yards backing fabric

King-size quilt batting

Cutting

Pattern for F triangle template is on page 174. Measurements include ¼" seam allowances. Follow manufacturer's instructions if using fusible web. Border strips are exact length needed. You may want to make them longer to allow for piecing variations.

From cream solid, cut:

• 1 (30⅞") square. Cut square in half diagonally in both directions to make 4 quarter-square A triangles.

• 4 (21½"-wide) strips. From strips, cut 4 (21½") B squares.

• 1 (6¼"-wide) strip. From strip, cut 4 (6¼") squares. Cut squares in half diagonally in both directions to make 16 quarter-square C triangles.

• 2 (3⅞"-wide) strips. From strips, cut 16 (3⅞") D squares.

• 2 (2⅝"-wide) strips for strip sets.

• 144 F triangles using template.

From tan print, cut:

• 29 (2⅝"-wide) strips for strip sets.

• 2 (2⅝"-wide) strips. From strips, cut 16 (2⅝") E diamonds.

Sew Smart

Cutting E diamonds:

Cut 2⅝"-wide strips. Trim end of strip at 45-degree angle. Lay 2⅝" line of ruler along angled side of strip. Cut along edge of ruler to make 1 E diamond. Continue cutting in this manner to make required number of E diamonds.

From brown print, cut:

• 5 (2⅝"-wide) strips for strip sets.

• 2 (2⅝"-wide) strips. From strips, cut 16 (2⅝") E diamonds.

• 12 (2¼"-wide) strips for binding.

From pink print, cut:

• 7 (2⅝"-wide) strips for strip sets.

From red print, cut:

• 26 (2⅝"-wide) strips for strip sets.

From light teal print, cut:

• 6 (2⅝"-wide) strips for strip sets.

From dark teal print, cut:

• 8 (2⅝"-wide) strips for strip sets.

From large-scale print, cut:

• 8 appliqué motifs.

From multi-color print, cut:

• 11 (6"-wide) strips. Piece strips to make 2 (6" x 112⅛") top and bottom outer borders and 2 (6" x 101⅛") side outer borders.

• 8 (4"-wide) strips. Piece strips to make 2 (4" x 79⅛") top and bottom inner borders and 2 (4" x 72⅛") side inner borders.

Center Assembly

1. Referring to *Strip Set 1 Diagram*, join 2 (2⅝"-wide) tan print strips and 1 (2⅝"-wide) strip each of brown print, pink print, red print, light teal print, and dark teal print as shown to complete Strip Set 1. Offset strips by about 2⅝". Trim left end of strip set at a 45-degree angle. Lay 2⅝" line on ruler atop angled cut. Cut along edge of ruler to cut a strip of joined diamonds that is 2⅝" wide. Cut 8 Strip Set 1 segments.

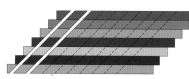

Strip Set 1 Diagram

2. In a similar manner, join strips as shown in *Strip Set Diagrams 2–7* to make remaining strip sets. Cut 8 (2⅝"-wide) segments from each strip set.

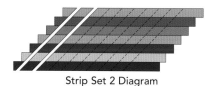

Strip Set 2 Diagram

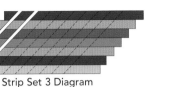

Strip Set 3 Diagram

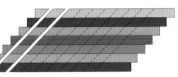

Strip Set 4 Diagram

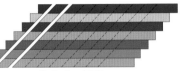

Strip Set 5 Diagram

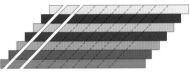

Strip Set 6 Diagram

Strip Set 7 Diagram

Referring to *Pieced Diagram Assembly Diagram*, lay out 1 each of segments #1–#7. Join segments to complete Pieced Diamond *(Pieced Diamond Diagram)*. Make 8 Pieced Diamonds.

1　2　3　4　5　6　7

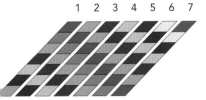

Pieced Diamond Assembly Diagram

Pieced Diamond Diagram

4. Lay out 8 Pieced Diamonds as shown in *Center Assembly Diagram*. Join diamonds to form a star. Set in 1 cream B square in each corner and 1 cream A triangle on each side of star.

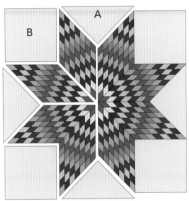

Center Assembly Diagram

5. Fuse appliqué motifs in A triangles and B squares. Use zigzag stitch and matching or invisible thread to stitch around motifs.

Pieced Border Assembly

1. Referring to *Strip Set 8 Diagram*, join 1 (2⅝"-wide) tan print strip and 1 (2⅝"-wide) red print strip to make Strip Set 8. Offset strips by about 2⅝" as shown. Make 17 strip sets. Trim left end of strip set at a 45-degree angle. Lay 2⅝" line on ruler atop angled cut. Cut along edge of ruler to cut a strip of joined diamonds that is 2⅝" wide. Cut 136 Strip Set 8 segments.

Strip Set 8 Diagram

2. Lay out 34 Strip Set 8 segments and 36 F triangles as shown in *Border Diagram*. Join into diagonal rows; join rows to complete border. Make 4 borders. Trim ends of border as shown in *Border Diagram*.

Border Diagram

Trim

Border Corner Assembly

1. Lay out 4 tan print E diamonds, 4 brown print E diamonds, 4 cream C triangles, and 4 cream D squares as shown in *Corner Block Assembly Diagram*.

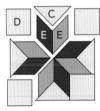

Corner Block Assembly Diagram

2. Join diamonds into a star. Set in cream C and D pieces to complete corner block *(Corner Block Diagram)*. C triangles and D squares are slightly oversized to make corner block the correct size (11½" unfinished). Make 4 corner blocks.

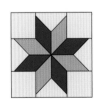

Corner Block Diagram

Quilt Assembly

1. Referring to *Quilt Top Assembly Diagram*, add side inner borders to quilt center. Add top and bottom inner borders to quilt.

2. Add 1 pieced border to each side of quilt center. Join 1 corner block to each end of remaining pieced borders. Add to top and bottom of quilt.

3. Add side outer borders to quilt top. Add top and bottom outer borders to quilt.

Finishing

1. Divide backing into 3 (3⅓-yard) pieces. Join panels lengthwise.

2. Layer backing, batting, and quilt top; baste. Quilt as desired. Quilt shown was outline quilted in the star and around appliqué, and has a grid in the background, oak leaves the pieced border, and diagonal line in the inner and outer borders.

3. Join 2¼"-wide brown print strip into 1 continuous piece for straight grain French-fold binding. Add binding to quilt.

Quilt Top Assembly Diagram

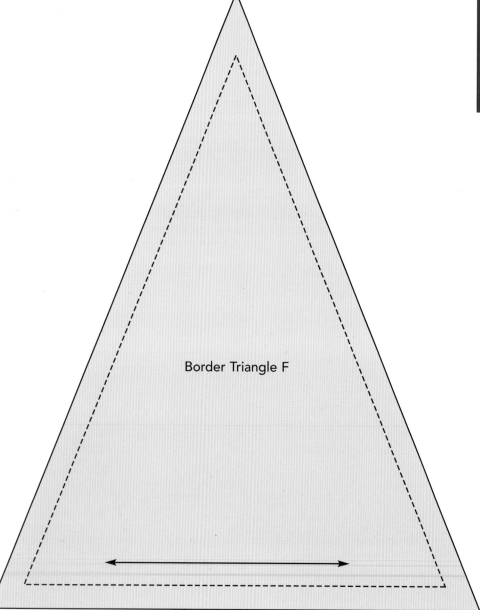

Border Triangle F

174

Star of Bethlehem Quilt

Quilts from
The Henry Ford

We love the orderliness of this finely crafted quilt. The zigzag border looks like a picket fence designed to keep the unruly peonies under control. This quilt is a perfect representative of nineteenth-century quilts that reflected the American woman's love of flowers.

——Liz

Peony Quilt

From earliest Colonial days, American quilters drew inspiration from the beauty of nature, especially the botanical world of trees, flowering vines, fruit, and above all, flowers. Dozens of motifs show stylized lilies, tulips, asters, daisies, or roses. Here, the peony is the star.

(*Note:* For the quilt projects, some of the dimensions and patterns may have been altered slightly to conform to today's cutting and piecing techniques.)

Peony

Diagonal sashing and a pieced border distinguish this *Peony* quilt, hand-sewn around 1850, possibly in Ohio. Flowers are pieced of red and green roller-printed calicoes in small abstracts; the stems are appliquéd. The quilting is 9 to 10 stitches to the inch, outline along the borders and sashing, "X" on the white ground of the blocks, and foliage among the peony stems.

Object ID: 55.55.4

Peony

PROJECT RATING: CHALLENGING
Size: 76⅝" x 97⅜"
Blocks: 18 (14") Peony blocks

Materials

7 yards white solid for blocks, borders, and binding
2⅜ yards red print for blocks and border
3½ yards green print for blocks and borders
6 yards backing fabric
Queen-size quilt batting

Cutting

Patterns for templates are on page 182. Measurements include ¼" seam allowances. Border strips are exact length needed. You may want to make them longer to allow for piecing variations.

From white solid, cut:

- 3 (5⅜"-wide) strips. From strips, cut 18 F pieces using template.
- 3 (4"-wide) strips. From strips, cut 28 (4") E squares.
- 4 (4½"-wide) strips. From strips, cut 60 (2½" x 4½") D rectangles.
- 18 (3¾"-wide) strips. From strips, cut 177 (3¾") squares. Cut squares in half diagonally in both directions to make 708 quarter-square C triangles.
- 1 (3⅜"-wide) strip. From strip, cut 2 (3⅜") squares. Cut squares in half diagonally to make 2 half-square I triangles.
- 1 (3"-wide) strip. From strip, cut 4 (3") squares. Cut squares in half diagonally in both directions to make 16 quarter-square N triangles.

- 8 (2¼"-wide) strips. From strips, cut 124 (2¼") B squares.
- 9 (2¼"-wide) strips for binding.
- 1 (1¾"-wide) strip. From strip, cut 16 (1¾") M squares.
- 30 (1½"-wide) strips. From strips, cut 60 (1½" x 14½") K rectangles and 36 (1½" x 12½") J rectangles.
- 4 (1⅜"-wide) strips. From strips, cut 18 (1⅜" x 6¾") H rectangles.
- 3 (1¼"-wide) strips. From strips, cut 8 (1¼" x 4¾") O rectangles and 8 (1¼" x 6¼") P rectangles.
- 16 (1¼"-wide) strips. Piece strips to make 2 (1¼" x 83⅞") side inner borders, 2 (1¼" x 64½") top and bottom inner borders, 2 (1¼" x 83⅞") side outer borders, and 2 (1¼" x 63") top and bottom outer borders.

From red print, cut:

- 7 (3¾"-wide) strips. From strips, cut 61 (3¾") squares. Cut squares in half diagonally in both directions to make 244 quarter-square C triangles.
- 30 (1¾"-wide) strips. From strips, cut 440 A diamonds. (See *Cutting Diamonds* on page 182.)
- 1 (1⅜"-wide) strip. From strip, cut 16 L diamonds. (See *Cutting Diamonds* on page 182.)

From green print, cut:

- 1 (18"-long) piece. From piece, cut about 460" of 1⅛"-wide bias strips. Join strips; press in thirds for stems. From pressed strips, cut 18 (10"-long) stems, 36 (6"-long) stems, and 14 (4"-long) stems.

- 7 (3¾"-wide) strips. From strips, cut 61 (3¾") squares. Cut squares in half diagonally in both directions to make 244 quarter-square C triangles.
- 1 (3⅜"-wide) strip. From strip, cut 9 (3⅜") squares. Cut squares in half diagonally to make 18 half-square I triangles.
- 5 (2¼"-wide) strips. From strips, using G template, cut 18 G diamonds and 18 G reverse diamonds.
- 13 (1¾"-wide) strips. From strips, cut 184 A diamonds. (See *Cutting Diamonds* on page 182.)
- 1 (1⅜"-wide) strip. From strip, cut 16 L diamonds. (See *Cutting Diamonds* on page 182.)
- 21 (1¼"-wide) strips. From strips, cut 24 (1¼" x 14½") short sashing strips and 2 (1¼" x 17") long sashing strips. Piece remaining strips to make 2 (1¼" x 47"), 2 (1¼" x 76"), and 1 (1¼" x 91") long sashing strips.
- 1 (1"-wide) strip. From strip, cut 4 (1" x 6¼") Q rectangles.
- 9 (1"-wide) strips. Piece strips to make 2 (1" x 77⅛") top and bottom middle borders and 2 (1" x 85⅜") side middle borders.

Block Assembly

1. Join 6 red print A diamonds and 2 green print A diamonds to make a Flower Unit *(Flower Unit Diagram)*. Make 3 Flower Units.

Flower Unit Diagram

Referring to *Assembly Diagram 1*, t in white B, C, and D pieces to in Flower Units.

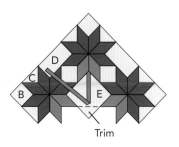

Assembly Diagram 1

. Baste 1 (10"-long) stem to corner f 1 E square. Set in E square etween Flower Units, catching stem seam. Trim bottom corner of E quare as shown.

. Baste 1 (6"-long) stem to each p corner of 1 F piece. With center em folded out of the way, set in 1 hite F piece between Flower Units s shown in *Assembly Diagram 2*, atching side stems in seams.

Assembly Diagram 2

. Join 1 white C triangle and 1 reen print G diamond to make Leaf Unit *(Leaf Unit Diagrams)*. oin 1 white C triangle and 1 G everse diamond to make 1 Reverse eaf Unit.

Leaf Unit Diagrams

6. Referring to *Assembly Diagram 3*, set in Leaf Units on sides of block.

Assembly Diagram 3

7. Referring to *Assembly Diagram 4*, join 1 H rectangle to bottom of block. Trim sides as shown.

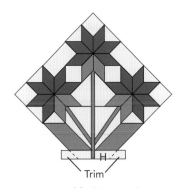

Assembly Diagram 4

8. Position stems on block and appliqué in place.

9. Referring to *Assembly Diagram 5*, join 1 green print I triangle to bottom of block, catching center stem in seam.

Assembly Diagram 5

10. Add J rectangles to 2 sides of block. Add K rectangles to remaining 2 sides to complete 1 Peony block *(Block Diagram)*. Make 18 blocks.

Block Diagram

Side Setting Triangle Assembly

1. Lay out pieces as shown in *Side Setting Triangle Diagram*. Join A diamonds into Flower Units. Set in white B, C, and D pieces to join Flower Units.

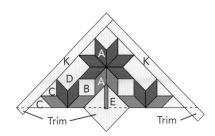

Side Setting Triangle Diagram

2. Baste 1 (4"-long) stem to corner of E square. Set in E square between Flower Units, catching stem in seam. Appliqué stem to background.

3. Join 1 K rectangle to each side of triangle. Trim K rectangles and E square as shown to complete 1 Side Setting Triangle. Make 10 Side Setting Triangles.

Corner Setting Triangle Assembly

1. Lay out pieces as shown in *Corner Setting Triangle Diagram*. Join A diamonds into partial Flower Units. Set in white B, C, and D pieces to join Flower Units.

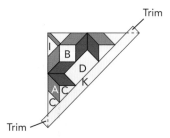

Corner Setting Triangle Diagram

2. Baste 1 (4"-long) stem to center of I triangle. Join I triangle to corner of unit, catching stem in seam. Appliqué stem to background.

3. Join 1 K rectangle to edge of triangle. Trim as shown to complete 1 Corner Setting Triangle. Make 4 Corner Setting Triangles.

Corner Block Assembly

1. Join 4 red print L diamonds and 4 green print L diamonds to make a Flower Unit.

2. Referring to *Corner Block Assembly Diagram*, set in white M and N pieces between diamonds.

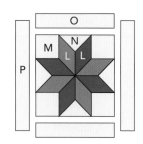

Corner Block Assembly Diagram

3. Add 1 O rectangle to top and bottom of block. Add 1 P rectangle to each side to complete Corner block (*Corner Block Diagram*). Make 4 Corner blocks.

Corner Block Diagram

Pieced Border Assembly

1. Referring to *Border Assembly Diagram*, join 34 red print C triangles and 35 white C triangles for Row 1. Join 35 green print C triangles and 34 white triangles for Row 2. Join 34 green print C triangles and 35 white triangles for Row 3. Join 35 red print C triangles and 34 white C triangles for Row 4.

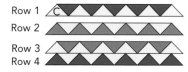

Border Assembly Diagram

2. Join rows as shown to complete 1 side border. Make 2 side borders.

3. Join 26 red print C triangles and 27 white C triangles for Row 1 of top border. Join 27 green print C triangles and 26 white triangles for Row 2. Join 26 green print C triangles and 27 white triangles for Row 3. Join 27 red print C triangles and 26 white C triangles for Row 4.

4. Join rows to complete top border. Repeat for bottom border.

Quilt Assembly

1. Lay out blocks, short sashing strips, and setting triangles as shown in *Quilt Top Assembly Diagram*. Join into diagonal rows.

2. Layout long sashing strips between diagonal rows; join rows and long sashing strips to complete quilt center. Trim sashing strips even with edges of quilt top.

3. Add white side inner borders to quilt center. Add white top and bottom inner borders to quilt.

4. Add green side middle borders to quilt top.

5. Trim 1 pieced side border to 83⅞" long. Referring to *Quilt Top Assembly Diagram*, join white side outer border to pieced border. Add 1 P rectangle to each end of border. Join border unit to side of quilt. Repeat for opposite side.

6. Add green top and bottom middle borders to quilt top.

7. Trim pieced top border to 63" long. Join white top outer border to pieced border. Add 1 P rectangle, 1 green Q rectangle, and 1 Corner block to each end of border. Join border unit to top of quilt. Repeat for bottom of quilt.

Finishing

1. Divide backing into 2 (3-yard) pieces. Divide 1 piece in half lengthwise to make 2 narrow panels. Sew narrow panel to each side of wider panel; press seam allowances toward narrow panels.

2. Layer backing, batting, and quilt top; baste. Quilt as desired. Quilt shown was outline quilted around the flowers, has a grid in the block background, and has straight lines parallel to the sides of the quilt in the borders.

3. Join 2¼"-wide white strips into 1 continuous piece for straight-grain French-fold binding. Add binding to quilt.

Quilt Top Assembly Diagram

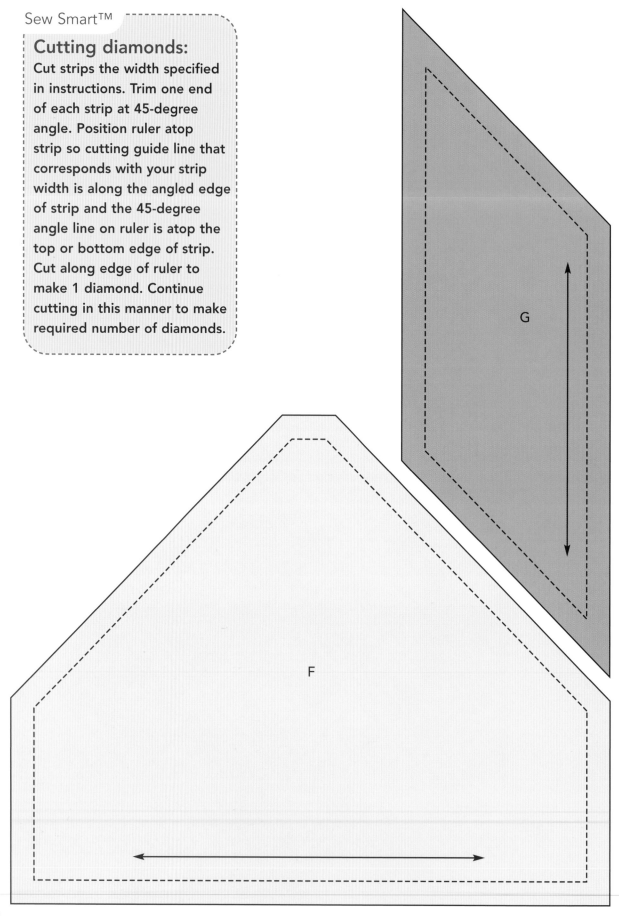

Cutting diamonds:
Cut strips the width specified in instructions. Trim one end of each strip at 45-degree angle. Position ruler atop strip so cutting guide line that corresponds with your strip width is along the angled edge of strip and the 45-degree angle line on ruler is atop the top or bottom edge of strip. Cut along edge of ruler to make 1 diamond. Continue cutting in this manner to make required number of diamonds.

G

F

Peony Quilt

We wonder—if the purpose of a quilt was simply to keep the family warm, why were patterns like Mariner's Compass and this Pineapple ever conceived? Simple squares, randomly joined, would have done the trick. Clearly, the women of nineteenth-century America had a desire to create patterns that were well satisfied by the possibilities inherent in printed cotton cloth.   ——Marianne

Pineapple Quilt

As a traditional symbol of hospitality, the

pineapple motif is often incorporated into vintage

home furnishings, including quilts. The complex

and dramatic Pineapple pattern (also known as

Windmill Blades), is built like the Log Cabin

pattern—rounds of strips are added to the

center square.

(*Note:* For the quilt projects, some of the dimensions and patterns may have
been altered slightly to conform to today's cutting and piecing techniques.)

Pineapple

This lightweight spread is neither
quilted nor tied. It is foundation
pieced by sewing machine. A dark
blue and white discharge print is
combined with a print of blue stars
on white ground and red and black
floral prints, all roller-printed. Two
sides have a strip border. The lack of
batting and the muslin backing
suggest summertime use.

Object ID: 74.128.5

Pineapple

Size: 77¼" x 88½"
Blocks: 30 (14¾") Pineapple blocks

Materials

3½ yards red print for blocks and outer border
3¼ yards dark blue print for blocks
1 yard light red solid for blocks
1 yard blue-on-white print for blocks
2½ yards cream print for blocks
3⅛ yards tan print for blocks, inner border, and binding
7⅛ yards backing fabric
Full-size quilt batting

Cutting

After cutting (1¼"-wide) strips for blocks, refer to *Cutting Chart* at right to cut required number of each piece. Because there are so many pieces which are similar in size, you may want to label them as you cut. Measurements include ¼" seam allowances. Border strips are exact length needed. You may want to make them longer to allow for piecing variations.

From red print, cut:
• 3 (3"-wide) strips. From strips, cut 30 (3") squares. Cut squares in half diagonally to make 60 half-square C triangles.
• 5 (1½"-wide) strips. Piece strips, to make 2 (1½" x 89") outer borders.
• 76 (1¼"-wide) strips for blocks.

From dark blue print, cut:
• 3 (3"-wide) strips. From strips, cut 30 (3") squares. Cut squares in half diagonally to make 60 half-square C triangles.
• 76 (1¼"-wide) strips for blocks.

From light red solid, cut:
• 4 (5"-wide) strips. From strips, cut 30 (5") squares. Cut squares in half diagonally to make 60 half-square R triangles.
• 2 (2⅝"-wide) strips. From strips, cut 30 (2⅝") A squares.

From blue-on-white print, cut:
• 4 (5"-wide) strips. From strips, cut 30 (5") squares. Cut squares in half diagonally to make 60 half-square R triangles.
• 4 (2⅜"-wide) strips. From strips, cut 60 (2⅜") squares. Cut squares in half diagonally to make 120 half-square B triangles.

From cream print, cut:
• 61 (1¼"-wide) strips for blocks.

From tan print, cut:
• 9 (2¼"-wide) strips for binding.
• 5 (1¼"-wide) strips. Piece strips to make 2 (1¼" x 89") inner borders.
• 61 (1¼"-wide) strips for blocks.

Cutting Chart for 1 Patchwork Pineapple Block					
PIECE	SIZE	RED PRINT	DK BLUE PRINT	CREAM PRINT	TAN PRINT
Q	1¼" x 8¾"	60	60		
P	1¼" x 7¼"			60	60
O	1¼" x 8"	60	60		
N	1¼" x 6½"			60	60
M	1¼" x 7½"	60	60		
L	1¼" x 6"			60	60
K	1¼" x 6¾"	60	60		
J	1¼" x 5¼"			60	60
I	1¼" x 6¼"	60	60		
H	1¼" x 4¾"			60	60
G	1¼" x 5½"	60	60		
F	1¼" x 4"			60	60
E	1¼" x 5"				
D	1¼" x 3½			60	60

Block Assembly

1. Lay out 1 light red A square, 4 blue/white B triangles, and 4 red print C triangles as shown in *Round 1 Diagrams*. Join pieces to complete Round 1.

Round 1 Diagrams

2. Referring to *Round 2 Diagrams*, add 1 tan print D rectangle to each side of block. Lay 1" line of ruler along seam line between B and C triangles. Cut along edge of ruler to trim block as shown.

Round 2 Diagrams

3. Referring to *Round 3 Diagrams*, add 1 dark blue print E rectangle to each side of block. Trim E rectangles even with D piece as shown.

Round 3 Diagrams

4. Continue adding rectangles and trimming as shown in *Round 4–Round 15 Diagrams*.

Round 4 Diagrams

Round 5 Diagrams

Round 6 Diagrams

Round 7 Diagrams

Round 8 Diagrams

Round 9 Diagrams

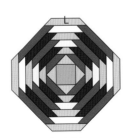

Round 10 Diagrams

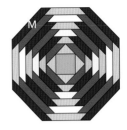

Round 11 Diagrams

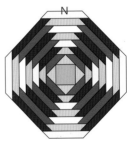

Round 12 Diagrams

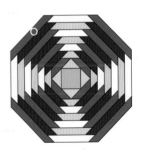

Round 13 Diagrams

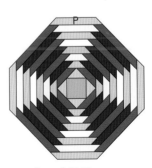

Round 14 Diagrams

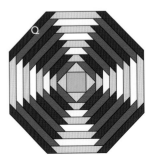

Round 15 Diagrams

5. Add 1 blue/white R triangle to each corner to complete 1 blue Pineapple block *(Blue Block Diagram)*. Make 15 blue blocks.

6. In a similar manner, make 15 red Pineapple blocks, reversing colors as shown in *Red Block Diagram*.

Quilt Assembly

1. Lay out blocks in 6 rows with 5 blocks in each, alternating colors shown in *Quilt Top Assembly Diagram*. Join blocks into rows; join rows to complete quilt center.

2. Join 1 tan print inner border strip and 1 red print outer border strip to make side border. Make 2 side borders. Add borders to quilt.

Finishing

1. Divide backing into 3 (2⅜-yard) pieces. Join pieces lengthwise. Seam will run horizontally.

2. Layer backing, batting, and quilt top; baste. Quilt as desired. Quilt shown was not quilted.

3. Join 2¼"-wide tan print strips into 1 continuous piece for straight-grain French-fold binding. Add binding to quilt.

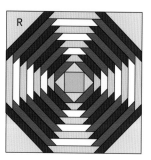

Blue Block Diagram

Red Block Diagram

Quilt Top Assembly Diagram

Pineapple Quilt

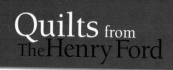

Beautiful in pink and white solids, just imagine this classic pattern done in scrap bag style, substituting dozens of dark scraps for the pink fabric and a myriad of shirting prints for the white.

———Liz

Lady of the Lake Quilt

While most of the quilt pattern names refer to the ordinaries of life, a few are named for literary works. *Lady of the Lake* commemorates Sir Walter Scott's famous poem, published in 1810. This geometric pattern became popular in the second quarter of the nineteenth century and has remained in use, still by its original (and only) name.

(*Note:* For the quilt projects, some of the dimensions and patterns may have been altered slightly to conform to today's cutting and piecing techniques.)

Lady of the Lake

Fabric choices that make this Gay Nineties quilt sparkle include the double pink floral calico in the piecing. The borders on two sides are pieced in sawtooth rows. The quilting, 5 stitches to the inch, is in concentric squares, in white thread. The top was made around 1895; the batting and backing may have some synthetic component, which would indicate that the quilt was finished at a later date.

Object ID: 00.3.16614

Lady of the Lake

Size: 69⅝" x 76½"
Blocks: 49 (9") Lady of the Lake blocks

Materials
5 yards white solid for blocks and binding
4½ yards pink solid for blocks
4¾ yards backing fabric
Full-size quilt batting

Cutting
Measurements include ¼" seam allowances.

From white solid, cut:
• 6 (6⅞"-wide) strips. From strips, cut 30 (6⅞") squares. Cut squares in half diagonally to make 60 half-square A triangles.
• 44 (2⅜"-wide) strips. From strips, cut 702 (2⅜") squares. Cut squares in half diagonally to make 1404 half-square B triangles.
• 8 (2¼"-wide) strips for binding.

From red solid, cut:
• 6 (6⅞"-wide) strips. From strips, cut 30 (6⅞") squares. Cut squares in half diagonally to make 60 half-square A triangles.
• 44 (2⅜"-wide) strips. From strips, cut 702 (2⅜") squares. Cut squares in half diagonally to make 1404 half-square B triangles.

Block Assembly
1. Join 1 white A triangle and 1 pink A triangle to make a triangle-square. Make 49 A triangle-squares.
2. Join 1 white B triangle and 1 pink B triangle to make a triangle-square. Make 1382 B triangle-squares.

3. Lay out 1 A triangle-square and 20 B triangle-squares as shown in *Block Assembly Diagram*. Join 4 B triangle-squares as shown; add to side of A triangle-square. Repeat for opposite side.

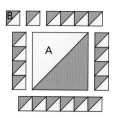

Block Assembly Diagram

4. Join 6 B triangle-squares; add to top of A triangle-square. Repeat for bottom to complete 1 Lady of the Lake block *(Block Diagram)*. Make 49 blocks.

Block Diagram

Setting Block Assembly
1. Lay out 1 pink A triangle, 9 B triangle-squares, and 2 white B triangles as shown in *Setting Block Assembly Diagram*. Join 4 B triangle-squares and 1 white B triangle as shown; add to left side of A triangle.

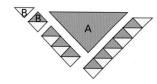

Setting Block Assembly Diagram

2. Join 5 B triangle-squares and 1 white B triangle; add to right side of A triangle to complete 1 pink setting block *(Setting Block Diagrams)*. Make 11 pink setting blocks.
3. In the same manner, make 11 white setting blocks.

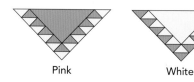

Pink   White
Setting Block Diagrams

Quilt Assembly
1. Lay out blocks as shown in *Quilt Top Assembly Diagram*. Join into diagonal rows; join rows to complete quilt center.
2. Join 51 B triangle-squares to make 1 side border strip. Make 4 side border strips.
3. Join 2 side border strips to complete 1 side border. Make 2 side borders. Add borders to quilt center.

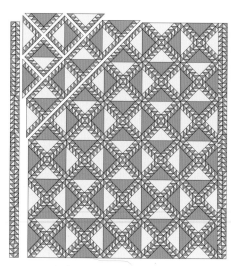

Quilt Top Assembly Diagram

Finishing

1. Divide backing into 2 (2⅜-yard) pieces. Divide 1 piece in half lengthwise to make 2 narrow panels. Sew 1 narrow panel to each side of wider panel; press seam allowances toward narrow panels.

2. Layer backing, batting, and quilt top; baste. Quilt as desired. Quilt shown was quilted with concentric squares.

3. Join 2¼"-wide white strips into 1 continuous piece for straight-grain French-fold binding. Add binding to quilt.

Lady of the Lake Quilt

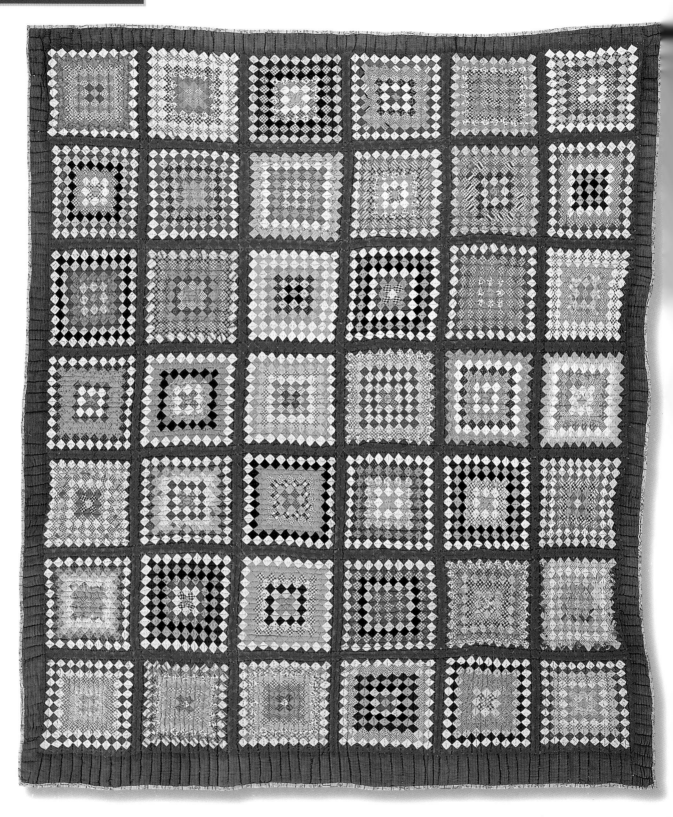

*The maker of this quilt, possibly Edna Martin, pieced the thousands of
tiny squares by hand, but you don't have to. Our instructions enable you
to construct the quilt with no set-in seams. You'll need to lay it all out,
preferably on a felt design wall, before you sew a single stitch.* ——Marianne

Postage Stamp Quilt

Sometime in the late nineteenth century, the Postage Stamp quilt became a popular format for competitive entries in displays at state and county fairs. Quilts that were recognized for having more than 10,000 tiny pieces were soon surpassed by works of art that contained several thousand more. The competitive trend later peaked with a Flower Basket quilt made from 87,789 pieces. This Postage Stamp was a blue-ribbon winner at the 1927 Alabama State Fair; it may have been made by Edna Martin of Wylan, Alabama, who presented it to the Henry Ford Museum.

(*Note:* For the quilt projects, some of the dimensions and patterns may have been altered slightly to conform to today's cutting and piecing techniques.)

Postage Stamp

The hand-sewn top is pieced with ¾" diamonds cut from solid colors and roller prints of many kinds; the dark blue strip border is semi-sheer cotton. The machine-sewn quilt backing is beige cotton, roller-printed with a lattice pattern of climbing roses.

Object ID: 27.311.1.1

Postage Stamp

PROJECT RATING: CHALLENGING
Size: 66½" x 73⅛"
Blocks: 42 (9½") Postage Stamp blocks

Materials

42 fat quarters★ assorted prints and solids for blocks
2½ yards dark blue solid for blocks and border
1 yard dark red solid for setting squares
⅝ yard floral print for binding
4¼ yards backing fabric
Twin-size quilt batting
★fat quarter = 18" x 20"

Cutting

Measurements include ¼" seam allowances. Border strips are exact length needed. You may want to make them longer to allow for piecing variations.

From each fat quarter, cut:
• 10 (1¼"-wide) strips. From strips, cut 145 (1¼") squares for blocks.

From dark blue solid, cut:
• 8 (2½"-wide) strips. Piece strips to make 2 (2½" x 73⅝") side borders and 2 (2½" x 67") top and bottom borders.
• 48 (1¼"-wide) strips. From strips, cut 1512 (1¼") squares for blocks.

From dark red solid, cut:
• 21 (1¼"-wide) strips. From strips, cut 669 (1¼") setting squares.

From floral print, cut:
• 8 (2¼"-wide) strips for binding.

Quilt Assembly

1. Lay out squares in concentric rows as shown in *Block Diagram*. Every block will have dark blue squares around outer edge. Referring to *Quilt Top Assembly Diagram*, lay out dark red setting squares between blocks. Quilt will be stitched in sections rather than in individual blocks.

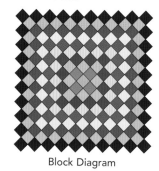

Block Diagram

2. Join squares into diagonal rows; join rows into sections as shown in *Quilt Top Assembly Diagram*. Join sections to complete quilt center.
3. Trim sides of quilt as shown to straighten.
4. Add side borders to quilt center. Add top and bottom borders to quilt.

Finishing

1. Divide backing into 2 (2⅛-yard) pieces. Join panels lengthwise. Seam will run horizontally.
2. Layer backing, batting, and quilt top; baste. Quilt as desired. Quilt shown was quilted with a grid of horizontal and vertical lines through the center of each square.
3. Join 2¼"-wide floral print strips into 1 continuous piece for straight-grain French-fold binding. Add binding to quilt.

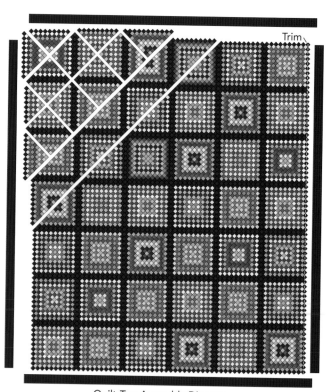

Quilt Top Assembly Diagram

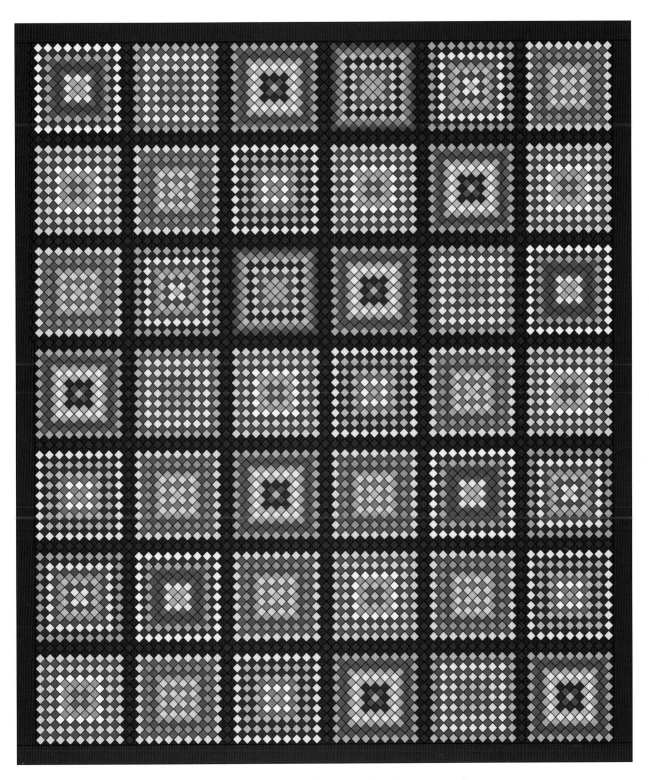

Postage Stamp Quilt

The power of wool solid fabrics is illustrated in this coverlet, which is not a true quilt, since it is tied rather than quilted. Exquisite hand embroidery enhances each fan, both at blade ends and the handle area. Luckily, more and more quilt shops are offering wool solids for quilters to add to their fabric stashes.

—Liz

Fancy Crazy Fan Quilt

The classic fan pattern is also called Fannie's Fan, Grandmother's Fan, or Japanese Fan. Sometimes only one corner of the block has a fan, sometimes two corners, and sometimes all the corners. Blocks can be arranged to display the pattern as single fans, as circles, or as miscellaneous fan blocks in a more varied "crazy" quilt block pattern. After the fan blocks are assembled, the top is often lavished with detailed embroidery.

(*Note:* For the quilt projects, some of the dimensions and patterns may have been altered slightly to conform to today's cutting and piecing techniques.)

Fancy Crazy Fan

Hand-sewn mainly in wool, this fan quilt is pieced, appliquéd, and embroidered. Floral motifs, including shamrocks, strawberries, and grapes, are embroidered in wool yarn along the circles and along the tops of the fans. The quilt's creator, Sarah Kirby (Mrs. Robert Kirby) of Vermontville, Michigan, was a farm wife. When she made this quilt in 1900, she was a widow who was running the farm with the help of her son's family. She died before the quilt was finished.

Object ID: 41.170.2

Fancy Crazy Fan

PROJECT RATING: INTERMEDIATE
Size: 78" x 91"
Blocks: 42 (13") Fan blocks

Materials
32 fat eighths★ assorted prints, plaids, and solids for fan blades
5¼ yards dark brown solid for background
⅝ yard tan solid for binding
7⅛ yards backing fabric
Queen-size quilt batting
★fat eighth = 9" x 20"

Cutting
Patterns to make templates are on page 201. Enlarge background pattern 200%. Measurements include ¼" seam allowances.

From each fat eighth, cut:
• 12 Blades.

From brown solid, cut:
• 42 Background pieces.
• 42 Center pieces.

From tan solid, cut:
• 9 (2¼"-wide) strips for binding.

Block Assembly
1. Choose 9 fan blade pieces and join as shown in *Block Assembly Diagram*.

Block Assembly Diagram

2. Place blade unit atop center piece, right sides facing. Stitch with ¼" seam. (See *Sew Easy: Making Nine-Blade Fan Units* on pages 205–206.)
3. Place background piece atop blade unit, right sides facing. Stitch with ¼" seam to complete 1 Fan block *(Block Diagram)*. Make 42 Fan blocks.

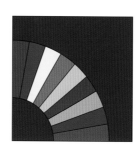

Block Diagram

Quilt Assembly
1. Lay out blocks as shown in *Quilt Top Assembly Diagram*.

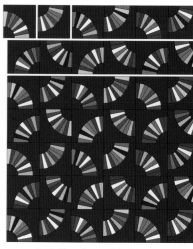

Quilt Top Assembly Diagram

2. Join into horizontal rows; join rows to complete quilt top.
3. Embellish blocks as desired with decorative embroidery stitches (see pages 202 and 203).

Finishing
1. Divide backing into 3 (2⅜-yard) pieces. Join panels lengthwise. Seams will run horizontally.
2. Layer backing, batting, and quilt top; baste. Quilt as desired. Quilt shown was not quilted.
3. Join 2¼"-wide tan strips into 1 continuous piece for straight-grain French-fold binding. Add binding to quilt.

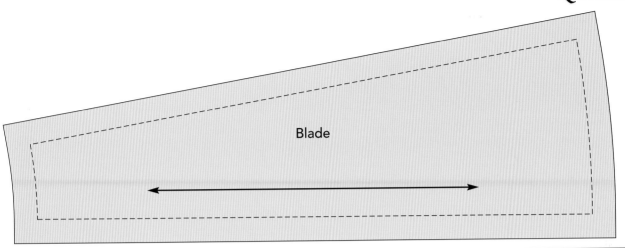

Blade

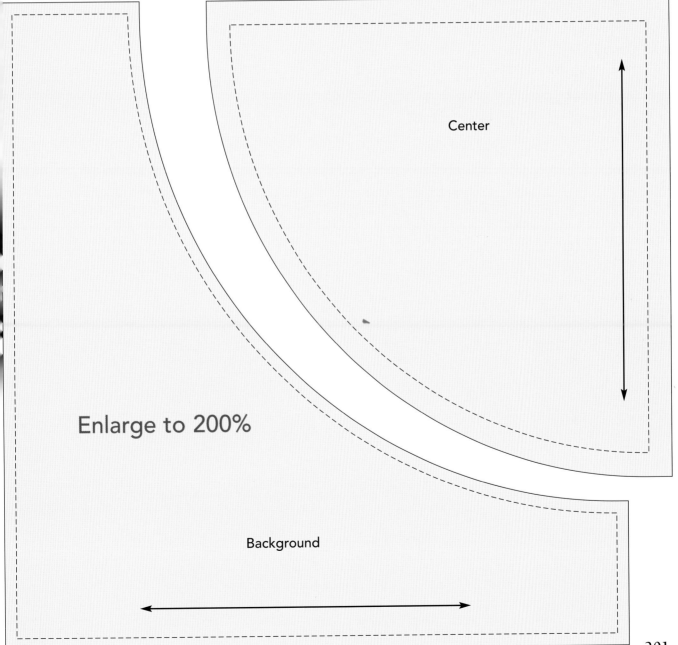

Center

Enlarge to 200%

Background

Embroidery

Each of the antique fans in the Fancy Crazy Fan quilt featured on page 198 is lavishly embroidered. Surprisingly enough, this amazing embellishment consists of only a few basic embroidery stitches. The standard stitches of today provided here are as close to the originals as possible. To complete the embroidery, begin by enlarging the embroidery pattern that shows the design and position of the stitches to 300 percent. As shown here, the pattern is drawn in full detail with an accompanying code—a number in a circle—that indicates the stitch that you will use to make a flower, leaf or stem. All the stitches used in the project are identified in the STITCHES box at right. Use three strands of embroidery floss, one strand of perle cotton or silk ribbon as desired.

Stitches

1. Feather
2. Herringbone
3. Satin
4. Stem
5. Straight

1. Feather

2. Herringbone

3. Satin

4. Stem

5. Straight

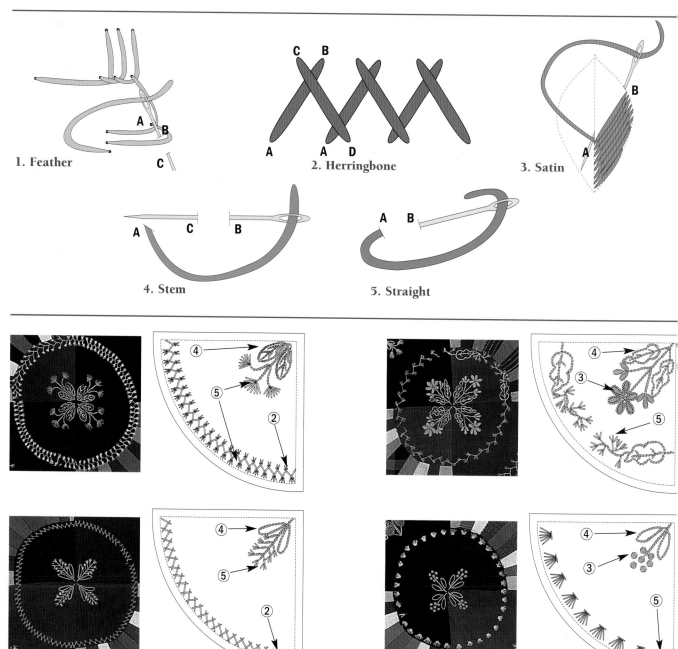

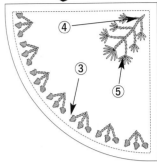

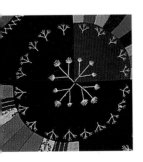

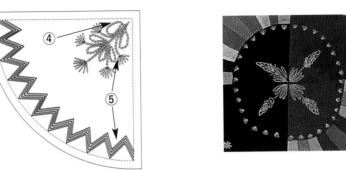

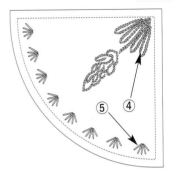

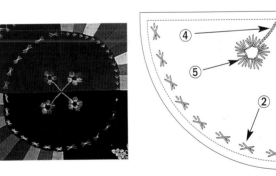

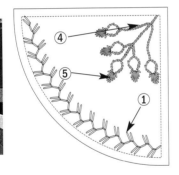

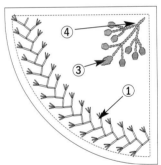

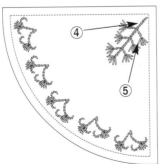

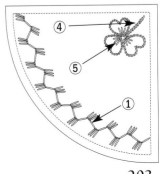

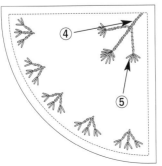

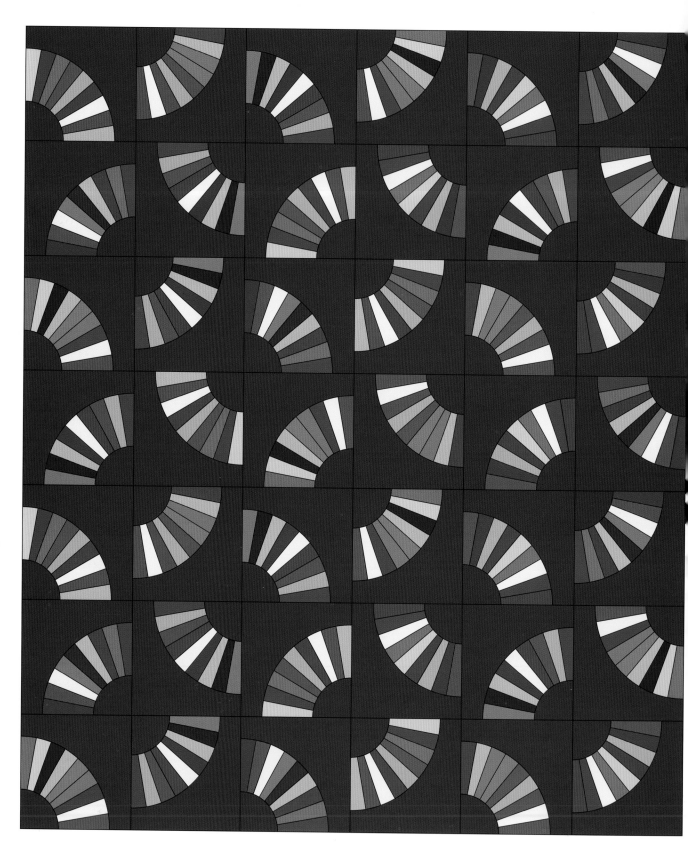

Fancy Crazy Fan Quilt

Making Nine-Blade Fan Units

Traditional fan blocks can be set in many different ways to make interesting designs. Stitch your fan blocks into the *Fancy Crazy Fan* quilt (page 198) or create a design of your own using the diagrams on page 206.

Cutting

1. Using center template, cut 1 center piece for each fan unit. Fold center piece in half and cut a tiny notch to mark center *(Photo A)*.

2. From background fabric, cut required number of background pieces, using template. Fold each background piece in half and cut a tiny notch to mark center *(Photo A)*.

3. Cut 9 blades for each fan unit, using template.

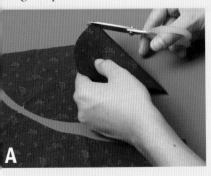

A

Assembly

1. Join 9 fan blades. Press all seam allowances in one direction *(Photo B)*.

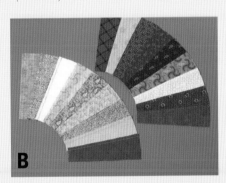

B

2. Place blade unit atop center piece, right sides together. Align center of blade unit with notch in center piece. Place a pin at each end and at notch in center piece *(Photo C)*.

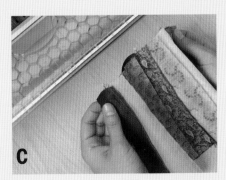

C

3. With blade unit on top, stitch ¼" seam *(Photo D)*. Press seam allowance toward center piece.

D

4. Place background piece atop blade unit, right sides together. Align center of blade unit with notch in background piece. Place a pin at each end and at notch in center of background piece. With background piece on top, stitch ¼" seam *(Photo E)*. Press seam allowance toward background piece.

E

Alternate Options for Nine-Blade Fan Units

We've come up with additional ways to set fan units to make interesting quilts. After you've made your blocks, try several different settings until you find one that's pleasing to you.

For Further Reading

Quilts and Quilting

Bresenhan, Karey Patterson, and Nancy O'Bryant Puentes. *Celebrate Great Quilts! Circa 1825–1940.* Lafayette, California: C&T Publishing, Inc., 2004.

Ferrero, Pat et al. *Hearts and Hands: The Influence of Women & Quilts on American Society.* San Francisco: The Quilt Digest Press, 1987.

Frye, L. Thomas, ed. *American Quilts: A Handmade Legacy.* Oakland, California: The Oakland Museum, 1981.

Katzenberg, Dena S. *Baltimore Album Quilts.* Baltimore: The Baltimore Museum of Art, 1981.

Kiracofe, Roderick, and Mary Elizabeth Johnson. *The American Quilt: A History of Cloth and Comfort.* New York: Clarkson Potter/Publishers, 2004.

Lasansky, Jeannette. *In the Heart of Pennsylvania: 19th and 20th Century Quiltmaking Traditions.* Lewisburg, Pennsylvania: Oral Traditions Project of the Union County (PA) Historical Society, 1985.

Lipsett, Linda Otto. *Remember Me: Women & Their Friendship Quilts.* San Francisco: The Quilt Digest Press, 1985.

McMorris, Penny. *Crazy Quilts.* New York: E. P. Dutton, Inc., 1985.

Orlofsky, Patsy and Myron. *Quilts in America.* New York: McGraw-Hill Book Company, 1974.

Snyder, Grace. *No Time on My Hands.* Lincoln, Nebraska: University of Nebraska Press, 1986.

Technology and American Society

Boorstin, Daniel J., et al. *Inventors and Discoverers: Changing Our World.* Washington, DC: The National Geographic Society, 1988.

Brinkley, Douglas. *Wheels for the World: Henry Ford, His Company, and a Century of Progress, 1903–2003.* New York: Viking, 2003.

Bryan, Ford R. *Henry's Attic: Some Fascinating Gifts To Henry Ford and His Museum.* Edited by Sarah Evans. Dearborn, Michigan: Ford Books, 1995.

Buehr, Walter. *Home Sweet Home in the 19th Century.* New York: Thomas Y. Crowell Company, Inc., 1965.

Cohen, Daniel. *Last Hundred Years: Household Technology.* New York: M. Evans & Co., 1982. (This is a book for young people.)

Constable, George, and Bob Somerville. *A Century of Innovations: Twenty Engineering Achievements That Transformed Our Lives.* Washington, DC: Joseph Henry Press, 2003.

Crouch, Tom D., and Peter L. Jakab. *The Wright Brothers and the Invention of the Aerial Age.* Washington, DC: Smithsonian Institution, 2003.

Davis, L. J. *Fleet Fire: Thomas Edison and the Pioneers of the Electric Revolution.* New York: Arcade Publishing Inc., 2003.

Evans, Harold. *They Made America: From the Steam Engine to the Search Engine.* New York: Little, Brown and Company, 2004.

Hardin, Wes; Pretzer, William S. and Steele, Susan M., eds. *An American Invention: The Story of Henry Ford Museum & Greenfield Village.* Ann Arbor, Michigan: University Litho, 1999.

Hardin, Wes. *The Henry Ford: A Pictorial Souvenir.* 4th Edition. Kansas City, Missouri: Terrell Creative, 2004.

Head, Jeanine M. and Pretzer, William S. *Henry Ford: A Pictorial Biography.* Revised Edition. Dearborn, Michigan: Henry Ford Museum & Greenfield Village, 1998.

Jonnes, Jill. *Empires of Light: Edison, Tesla, Westinghouse, and the Race to Electrify the World.* New York: Random House, 2003.

Karwatka, Dennis. *Technologies Past: America's Industrial Revolution and the People Who Delivered the Goods.* Ann Arbor, Michigan: Prakken Publications Inc., 1996.

Kauffman, Henry J. *The American Farmhouse.* New York: Hawthorn Books Inc., 1975.

Matteucci, Marco. *History of the Motorcar.* New York: Crown Publishers, 1970.

Mintz, Steven, and Susan Kellogg. *Domestic Revolutions: A Social History of American Family Life.* New York: The Free Press (a division of MacMillan, Inc.), 1988.

Mueller, Mike. *Ford: 100 Years.* St. Paul, Minnesota: Motorbooks International, 2003.

The front facade of *Henry Ford Museum* includes a full-sized replica of Philadelphia's Independence Hall. By duplicating this historic structure, Ford incorporated one of the best-known symbols of American freedom into a building designed to celebrate the accomplishments of American innovators.